Sifism

The Sufi Path
of
Annihilation

The Sufi Path

of

Annihilation

>-·-<

IN THE TRADITION OF
Mevlana Jalaluddin Rumi
and Hasan Lutfi Shushud

Nevit O. Ergin

Inner Traditions
Rochester, Vermont • Toronto, Canada

Inner Traditions
One Park Street
Rochester, Vermont 05767
www.InnerTraditions.com

Text stock is SFI certified

Library of Congress Cataloging-in-Publication Data

Ergin, Nevit O.
  The Sufi path of annihilation : in the tradition of Mevlana Jalaluddin Rumi and
Hasan Lutfi Shushud / Nevit O. Ergin.
      pages cm
  Includes bibliographical references.
  ISBN 978-1-62055-274-2 (pbk.) — ISBN 978-1-62055-275-9 (e-book)
  1. Fana' (Sufism) 2. Sufism—Doctrines. 3. Mysticism—Islam. 4. Jalal al-Din
Rumi, Maulana, 1207–1273. 5. Shushud, Hasan Lutfi. I. Title.
  BP189.3.E74 2014
  297.4'46—dc23

                                                                    2013036940

Printed and bound in the United States by Lake Book Manufacturing, Inc.
The text stock is SFI certified. The Sustainable Forestry Initiative® program
promotes sustainable forest management.

10 9 8 7 6 5 4 3 2 1

Text design and layout by Priscilla Baker
This book was typeset in Garamond Premier Pro with Gill Sans and Cochin used
as display typefaces

To send correspondence to the author of this book, mail a first-class letter to the
author c/o Inner Traditions • Bear & Company, One Park Street, Rochester, VT
05767, and we will forward the communication, or contact the author directly at
http://nevitergin.com.

Hasan Shushud in 1967, Cranbrook, Michigan

In memory of my dear master, Hasan Shushud

►•◄

O my God, make me obliged to You.
Introduce me to Fenâ [Annihilation].
Reach me to Baka [Nothingness].
Bless me by the Glory of Ke-en Lem Yekün
   [As if it had never happened].

HASAN LUTFI SHUSHUD

Fate is not the slave of heart's desire.
Existence is a means to reach Absence.
Our nanny is behind the curtain.
In fact, we are not here; those are our shadows.

MEVLANA JALALUDDIN RUMI

Contents

►•◄

►•◄

►•◄

Opening the Door
to Absence

Nevit O. Ergin

This book is not intended to interfere with the pleasures of life here and now, nor is it intended to question the validity of any conflict of any size or shape.

This book humbly attempts to address the eternal ignorances of the origin of life (birth), the end of life (death), and the in-between.

Since all roads eventually end up on a dead-end street . . . since, in the words of Mevlana, we build constantly mud houses on the water, is life really worth living?

Nevertheless, life is very precious. We have as our only capital, our body.

This book presents a possible alternative to this dilemma. Instead of wasting life in time, throwing our body into the ground, it describes a way to go beyond time to immortality, a way to work with the body to reach Absence.

My special thanks to Millicent Alexander, Andrew Moyer, and Meral Ekmekçioğlu for all of their support and dedication. Without them, this project would never have been born.

Either be Iranian or Rum or Turk.
Learn the language of the Mute.

MEVLANA JALALUDDIN RUMI

From Gölpinarli's *Dîvân-i Kebîr Mevlânâ Celâleddin,*
volume VII, Mütekaarib Maksür,
"Mefülü mefâilün feûlün," page 662, verse 8787

Meeting with Hasan Shushud

>-·-◄

Nevit O. Ergin

I was a young man traveling from Istanbul by bus with an acquaintance. It would be two hours before we were due to arrive at a small town at the northern part of the Bosporus. During this time I did all the talking. My companion, a middle-aged man who was dressed in an elegant, business-like way, listened. A few times the name of a mutual friend was mentioned. He had recently passed away and just before his death had asked this gentleman to introduce me to the person we were about to visit. My gentleman friend had promised to do so.

The person we were to meet was named Hasan L. Shushud. I knew nothing about him except that on a few occasions when I was fasting and trying to hold my breath intentionally for a minute or two (I was doing this out of desperation and curiosity), this mutual friend mentioned the name of a person, adding, "He would certainly like to meet you." He said nothing more than that. I didn't think he would take this so seriously, like a last will at the end of his life.

I was a young, arrogant snob, interested in metaphysics, literature, and philosophy. I knew a lot of people, but they were mostly artists, poets, and self-made philosophers whom I spent endless hours with, drinking wine and arguing new philosophical ideas of Europe or religious dogmas of the Middle East.

One of my acquaintances was a theater critic who told me that one day his brother would like to meet me. The brother turned out to be a bank executive who belonged to an entirely different world, but felt he had a mission to introduce me to his friend.

When we arrived at the house, which was very little and old and situated next to a small shrine with a white marble building, which made everything more interesting, a rather elderly, thin, white-haired man opened the door. He was well dressed and apparently waiting for us. With a faint smile he invited us in. Just before he closed the door, I noticed he looked up and down the street as if trying to see if anyone was watching us.

The house was meticulously clean, well decorated with old antique furniture, carpets, and curtains, which were drawn. On the small tables were valuable lamps, and there was a library packed full of old books.

He wanted me to sit next to him, almost within arm's reach. I noticed his eyes, withdrawn, but very deep, dark, and powerful. In his oval-shaped face his eyebrows were bushy, the lips very narrow, and they carried a most beautiful, meaningful, intelligent smile. He spoke very softly and I noticed there were long pauses when he finished a sentence as if he was catching his breath. Later, I saw his face contract with a light spasm and a few drops of tears come after such a long, breathless period.

If nothing else had been spoken that day, I knew at least one thing: When one holds his breath, I knew what would happen at the end. But on him this was spontaneous. After a few words about our deceased friend, he said I could ask some questions.

If I had been somewhere else or someone else, I would have been glad to throw in many questions. But that day in that particular house, in front of this unusual man, I had a hard time finding any. Instead of asking questions, I started telling him about the books I had read, and mentioned several names that had influenced me. His look disappointed me, but I went on and on, telling all my frustrations. He was listening patiently, which made me aware of how trivial my talking was. I looked at the person who had brought me here and was now sitting silently, begging his help, wanting him to say something to save me. He just sat there silently.

Our host understood my situation. He reached out to my hand, looked in my eyes, and said, "Have you ever thought, there are more things than books and people can ever give you?" Then softly he added, "You can reach new perception beyond yourself."

I asked, "How?"

He smiled with his eyes half-closed. "You'll know when the time comes."

"When?" I asked again.

"Just the way the days end and night comes, seasons change, trees and flowers blossom, and grass grows." Then, he added with that half-shy smile, "gradually, naturally." He then asked me, "I hear you do fasting and holding your breath. How did you start?"

I tried to summarize the events that had eventually led me into fasting. "All the talks, books, and schools haven't changed me. It doesn't matter if I think I exist, or I exist, then I think. I want more than that. I am tired of all this mental buffoonery."

He corrected me, "Mental abstraction. You want bodily abstraction."

I looked at his face with a big question mark.

He said, "Yes, it is possible. You were born with talent, which is passive. You have to work for it, which is active. All I can suggest and promise you is lots of hunger, breathlessness, and when the time comes, you will go through a hell of suffering. This road of Itlak is paved with fire, which burns you while you travel it." He paused and looked at me with those half-closed eyes, then after another period of breathlessness said, "This is not what you know. This is the way of Annihilation, Extinction."

That was the first time I had heard these words used that way. I was totally lost.

He understood my confusion. He reached to my hand again. "Son," he said softly, "don't be discouraged with all these big words. With patience, with persistence, and with the help of God, you'll experience them all."

I asked him again if there was anything I should read, just to get my Self familiarized with myself. He looked at me rather disappointedly. "Well," he said, "I'll send you a couple of pages if you leave your address."

When we left, I had no idea what I was getting into.

I spoke very little with my companion. He was just happy to see his mission accomplished.

But I felt mine was just beginning.

A few days later, I received an envelope from Mr. Shushud. Inside were two typed pages of his writings, the book I had forgotten and left at his house, and a short note.

"I didn't ask your permission, but I am answering some of the questions in this book. I hope you'll read it. You can stop by some Sunday at my house."

The book I had accidently left at his house was *The Prophet* by Khalil Gibran. In Hasan Shushud's handwritten note, he had taken liberties with the text of this book by devising similar questions to those posed in *The Prophet,* and penning his own answers to those questions.

A Poet said,
Tell us about beauty.
And he answered.
Reach the Absence.
You won't need all the beauty.

An old monk said,
Tell us about Religion.
He answered,
Reach the Source of Religion.
You'll be exempt from Religion.

It is time, they said,
To question you about Death.
And he answered,
You are such
That Life and Death
Are your appearances.

A young woman asked,
Tell us about suffering.
And he answered
Nothing but suffering can purify us.

Somebody asked,
Tell us about our faults,
And he answered,
Your faults and virtues don't count
    for much.

A teacher asked,
Tell us about teaching.
And he answered,
It is not by teaching or learning.
It is by annihilation.

A young man asked,
Tell us of friendship.
He answered,
The one who really knows Himself
Is in love with Himself.

An astronomer asked,
Tell us about time, oh, saint.
And he answered,

If you don't experience timelessness,
You don't know time.

An elder of the town asked,
Tell us about good and bad.
And he answered,
Bad belongs to your existence.
Good is your nothingness.

One of the priests asked,
Tell us about prayer.
And he answered,
Prayers are evidence of weakness and
    incompleteness.
Have you forgotten your divine destiny?

Then, a visitor, who came to town once
    in a while asked,
Tell us about pleasure.
And he answered,
The only pleasure of Earth
Is the detachment from Earth.

A young bride asked,
Tell us about marriage.
And he answered,
Marriage is the collision of two universes.

And the mother who held a babe in her
    arms asked,
Tell us about babies.
And he answered,
Your children are nothing but your extensions.

A rich man asked,
Tell us about giving.
And he answered,
You cannot give anything,
Even if you try to give Earth and Heaven,
They are illusions.

And the grocer asked,
Tell us about food.
And he answered,
Fasting is the food of saints and prophets.

The two-page letter was not as easy to decipher. Although it was typed in Turkish, I had read it, then read it again, but still couldn't understand it.

I was a university graduate and thought I was very literate, but this writing was full of old Turkish, which is full of old Arabic-Farsi terms, and the content was extremely abstract.

All I could understand was fasting and some kind of breathing were essential. Books and discussions were not. I didn't understand much of anything about the suffering. Subconsciously, I didn't want to get into it so much and I just left that part alone.

I showed the letter to some of my close friends. They didn't understand it either. One asked me if he could show it to his uncle. "Maybe," he said, "he could explain it to us." His uncle was an expert in these kinds of matters.

A couple of days later, he brought Mr. Shushud's letter back and told me his uncle was very much impressed and wondered how come the person who wrote this letter and who was obviously at a very, very high level of Sufism would send it to some novice like me.

I wondered that, too. I realized I should keep silent and save the letter and any further communications from Mr. Shushud.

I still wasn't sure what it was all about. I was familiar with fasting because in this country, Turkey, one month of fasting is a common occurrence for most of the people. They just don't eat or drink anything until sunset. Then they have everything they desire to eat or drink until they sleep. Even extending this type of fasting for a period longer than a month—if the person can tolerate it—is not an extraordinary concept. After several months, I had adjusted to this style of daily fasting without any hardship.

I didn't know any special way of breathing. I used to breathe rather fast and deep for a period of half a minute, then hold my breath as long as I could, which was sometimes one and a half to two minutes.

What other requirements were needed for the way of Itlak? I could hardly wait for the following Sunday to ask Mr. Shushud.

When I arrived, his room was very crowded. There was hardly a place to sit. He was very kind, brought a chair, and again had me sit very close to him.

I was the youngest guest in the room. The others were middle-aged or older. There were a few women, but most were men. They seemed to know each other.

Again, he was answering questions rather than giving a formal speech or lecture. Some of the people were writing down his answers.

I kept quiet, though I didn't understand most of the conversation. I also recorded some of his answers. (Thank God, I kept doing that for the rest of our meetings, which became historically important to me later.)

Mr. Shushud was very patient, extremely modest, and he went out of his way to make everyone feel most important and welcome.

When we were all ready to leave, I felt sorry that I hadn't understood most of the conversation. I was extremely comfortable and happy there. Also, I couldn't help but be amazed at all these hours of informal conversations with no earthly, moral advice, or any sign of sermon, formality, or hierarchy.

No requirements other than fasting and breathing were mentioned.

He quietly told me, just before I went out the door, "Son, I apolo-

Nevit Ergin and Hasan Shushud in 1967,
Cranbrook, Michigan

gize that I couldn't talk to you personally. Next time, instead of Sunday,
you come on Saturday."

I was so happy, I wanted to kiss his hand. Instead, he kissed mine.

On the bus, I sat next to one of the elderly guests. He was well over
seventy. He asked me how long I had known Mr. Shushud. I told him I
had known him for just about a week.

He looked in my eyes and said, "Do you know how lucky you are?"

I didn't answer.

He continued, "I have known Mr. Shushud for the last forty years.

We started almost together. I am now the same, except much older, but he has changed. I have probably read more books and listened to more talks. He did something else. I'm sorry I didn't do the same." Then he corrected himself, "I couldn't do it."

"But," I said, "you are still interested. You will eventually."

"No," he answered, shaking his head. "It is too late. Maybe next time."

I didn't specifically ask him what he meant. Did he believe in reincarnation? What was the thing he would do differently if he had a second chance?

Somehow, I felt lucky to have met such a remarkable man as Mr. Shushud. I was twenty-six years old then. It was the beginning of a lifelong relationship.

Editor's Note

►•◄

Hasan Shushud radiates from this book and also shines luminously through its two other accounts of him: one found in the book's center, a touchstone on your way, and the other account at its end. Each will give you further insights into this remarkable man and teacher. In between and all around, you will encounter stories written by Nevit Ergin, as well as various sayings and poems* that articulate the tenets of Itlak.

The dreaminess that they proffer is offset by very practical questions and Ergin's attempts to answer them (even though, in his view, there really *are* no questions—as you will discover yourself if you follow the path). At the end of the book, for the inquisitive reader, some additional biographical information on Mevlana Jalaluddin Rumi, Hasan Lutfi Shushud, and Nevit O. Ergin can be found.

May this book's sweet, otherworldly bouquet cast an indelible spell and entice you to learn more about the wonders of Itlak.

---

*The translations shared here are from the *Divân-i Kebîr,* registered under the numbers 68 and 69 in the Mevlana Museum in Konya, Turkey. Its 44,829 verses (contained in two volumes) were compiled in 1368. Its original language is the thirteenth-century Farsi spoken in Anatolia.

PART 1

On Sainthood and Prophethood

Sayings

Poems

A Story: Gospel without Apostle

Questions and Answers about Sainthood and Prophethood

Sayings

Hasan Lutfi Shushud

Although the religious associations and locations of Saints and Prophets can be problematic, one could easily realize that they are not ordinary people. They don't work for wealth, success, and happiness for themselves. Instead they do for others.

Sainthood is given to one who has annihilated "self."[1]

Sainthood is above the level of Prophethood. Some prophets have also acquired sainthood.[2]

But generally speaking, Prophethood is cheap, while annihilation is costly.[3]

Every saint has the informative or communicative function of prophecy.[4]

The individuals who were born with a "saintly disposition" "manifest weariness of being" [*vücûd bizarliği*] in their early ages. Instead of walking dead-end streets, these Divine misfits stay away from the existential coma. When the time comes, they will meet the "right teacher" and pursue the real journey of Annihilation [*fenâ*]. This is the escape from the dungeon of existence.[5]

The seeker who possesses this disposition will sooner or later achieve sainthood through steadfast striving on this path.[6]

But at a higher level of perception, one will be free from Prophethood as well as Sainthood.[7]

"Self" is born and dies. It is always in the hand and mercy of fate. The self is the source of all kinds of troubles, individual, national, international. This is a common knowledge of saints and prophets. How to annihilate the self? It is a technical matter, and it is a long journey.

Poems

Mevlana Jalaluddin Rumi

God made a revelation: O, my Messenger, He said,
Don't sit anywhere but next to lovers.
Although your fire warms the whole world,
Once it is covered by ashes, it will be extinguished.[8]

St. John of the Cross

Alas, who can ever heal me?
Oh, that you, my God,
May ever fully surrender yourself in truth to me.
Do not, I beg you, send any longer
Messengers who take your place
And do not know enough to tell my needs!

A Story

Gospel without Apostle

Nevit O. Ergin

I woke up to the sound of a vacuum cleaner. It was 5:00 in the morning. I dashed out of my room. It was the Colonel vacuuming the living room.

"What's going on?" I asked. He noticed my annoyance.

"The Commander is coming at 4:00 this afternoon. I'm getting ready for his inspection." His voice was very serious.

I couldn't help but ask, "Why now?"

"Sonny, he is very meticulous."

He liked to call me Sonny, even though my name wasn't Sonny. I used to call him Colonel, but his name was Sanford. He was my grandfather, and we lived together. All I knew about him was that he was a retired colonel, a veteran of all kinds of wars. Later he got a dog, named him Sanford, and he became "Colonel" to everyone.

"Can I go back to sleep?" I pleaded.

"Sure, Sonny. Please get up at 8:00. We have a whole day ahead of us. I am enlisting you to help me prepare for the inspection." He looked at my face and added, "Besides gaining the honor, you'll be well compensated."

When I got up at 9:00, the Colonel wasn't in the house. I found him in the backyard watering the plants. This was an every-morning ritual. He stopped at every tree and plant, looking at them, touching them, and talking to them before watering. A neighborhood black cat followed him faithfully during this inspection. While he filled the bird feeder with sunflower seeds, a few hungry squirrels and birds circled around.

He addressed them seriously. "You guys pretend to do what comes natural to you, but no killing here. Do you hear me?" When I asked him once what would come natural to them, he replied, "I feed them, Sonny. There's no reason for them to eat each other." He added, "Man is the one who kills for no reason."

"Colonel, who is coming?" I asked.

"I don't know his name, but he's the top of the top. The head guy," he replied.

"How do you know he's coming?"

"I saw him in my dream last night. He had so many stars, I couldn't even count them. Someone yelled, 'Attention,' so I stood at attention. 'Colonel,' he said, 'be ready tomorrow for inspection.'" My grandfather's voice was trembling. I knew just remembering the dream made him excited.

But I couldn't help asking, "Why you?"

"I don't know," he answered. "I was told he was looking for someone to help him."

The Colonel wanted to be sure everything was in perfect shape. He washed his car Blondie—a fifteen-year-old maroon Corolla. She was shining under the sun by the time he finished.

"Sonny," he said, "before the Commander comes, we have a few chores to do. Blondie's oil needs to be changed, I need to get a haircut, and then our shirts need to be picked up from the dry cleaners."

I did the driving; he sat next to me. The barber, service station, and dry cleaners were all in the same shopping center. The owners of these places were all familiar to him. We left the car at the service station and walked to the barbershop. It was a little room around the back with a small barber sign next to the door. The barber, an old, fragile man, greeted the Colonel. There was a customer in the chair; many pictures of old airplanes were on the wall. The Colonel told me he used to be in the Air Force.

After the customer left, the Colonel sat in the chair. He started the conversation, "First thing, how is your son?"

"He's still in jail," the barber replied. I later learned that his young son, who had mental problems, had assaulted his neighbors. They locked him up and he was awaiting trial. The barber explained, "I'm telling the public defender, 'this guy is sick, he needs his medication, his doctor.' But no one will listen. They say it will take time to see a doctor. I wish I could get a good attorney for him. He doesn't have money. Neither do I."

Then the Colonel asked exactly what I was afraid he would ask: "How much?" The barber stopped cutting his hair. "Come on now, Colonel, you can't do that, I can't ask that from you. Besides, you don't have the money." I was going to tell him he was right, but the Colonel insisted.

The barber told him he didn't know how much an attorney would cost for a case like that but he said he'd find out.

After the haircut, just before we left, the Colonel gave the barber one hundred dollars. Later I said, "That was a very expensive haircut." He didn't reply.

We then went to the dry cleaners. A Chinese woman gave us my shirts, but she couldn't find the Colonel's. That moving rail turned and turned, stopping time by time. They searched all over, but the Colonel's shirts were nowhere to be found. The Chinese lady was getting frustrated, and after ten minutes she gave up.

"Sir," she said hopelessly, "I can't find them." The Colonel was watching all of this, feeling very sorry for her. "Don't worry, it happens to all of us. What's our bill?"

"I'll charge you for his shirts and buy you two new ones," she said apologetically.

"No, no," the Colonel insisted, "you don't buy me anything. I'll pay for the laundry of my shirts." Despite the woman's resistance, he paid for everything.

The car was ready at the service station. With the oil change and new filters, the bill came to around forty dollars. The owner and the Colonel exchanged a few jokes, and we started on our way home. After a few miles, I heard some noises coming from the engine. I mentioned it to the Colonel, but he just said, "It's the new oil." The noises got louder and the smell of burnt oil filled the car. I turned back and we barely made it to the service station. We found out that after emptying out the dirty oil, the mechanic had forgotten to put in the new oil. He said it was a serious problem now and we'd have to leave the car.

The owner was blaming the mechanic, but the Colonel said, "He didn't do it intentionally. We shouldn't make him feel guilty." The owner looked at my face, and I looked at him. The mechanic left. I asked how long it would take. The owner said he would call us. He offered to charge only for parts and not labor, and the Colonel agreed immediately. The owner then took us home.

While resting in the backyard, I said, "What a day. Can we take Sanford for a walk on the beach?" Taking the dog for a walk on the beach was always the Colonel's routine.

We were late; the early spring coolness was in the air. After walking on the levy with Sanford, who was on a leash all the time, the Colonel sat in the place he always sat. There was a low tide; the sea was at least a hundred yards out from the beach. Pockets of seawater had been left behind, leaving all kinds of moss, weeds, and small creatures along the sand. There were birds of all shapes and sizes helping themselves.

The Colonel looked at the "killing field," as he called it. I didn't see it that way; they were feasting. "There's got to be a better way," he said. He never believed the most Benevolent Almighty set the survival of the species as a predator-prey relationship. The Colonel created microcosms of the Universe with labor and sacrifices in his backyard, feeding the birds and the animals and watering the plants. He probably knew his Utopia was his selfish dream; he should have no right to extend this behavior to the real world.

He took the leash off the dog and let Sanford free. Without hesitation, the dog ran down the levy, directly toward the beach. The Colonel was surprised and watched the dog rush toward the birds. A flock of small birds took off. Sanford did not stop; without changing direction he ran toward other birds. Now his body was half in the sea, and he was jumping up and down in order to run. The Colonel realized the danger of the unstable sand the dog was trying to run on.

"Sanford, come back home," he yelled. But the dog kept running until he became a small black dot on the sea and disappeared. The Colonel's voice was weak and hoarse, then he stopped yelling. We became speechless, standing, sad, looking at the horizon. The sea was calm and looked innocent and beautiful. It was only a short while ago when it had opened its mouth and swallowed the dog.

When we came home, tired and frustrated, we found a big envelope at the door addressed to the Colonel. There was no stamp and no return address. When I picked it up, I thought it was an announcement or advertisement, so I put it on the table to throw away later.

It was 3:00 in the afternoon. "We have an hour before the Commander arrives," the Colonel said. He wanted to take a shower to refresh himself, and I went to lie down for a short rest.

When we got together, it was close to 4:00. He had dressed up in his uniform, putting on all his medals. He looked relaxed and ready. I wondered about this so-called inspection, but I was also anxious to see the Commander.

Time passed and neither of us talked. We waited to hear footsteps, a doorbell. But nothing happened. At about 5:00, I dared to ask, "Are you sure he told you he was coming?"

He calmly replied, "Yes, Sonny, today at 4:00 p.m."

"In your dream?" I asked again.

"Yes, Sonny, in my dream."

We stayed in silence for another hour. The room was getting darker. "Maybe he has another appointment," I said.

With complete confidence he replied, "No, Sonny. Where is that envelope we found at the door?"

I had completely forgotten about it. I brought him the letter, adding, "It looks like junk mail."

He carefully opened the envelope and put on his reading glasses. He read carefully by himself. I could see his face was tense at first, but later a faint smile came and he relaxed. He was shaking his head with wonder. After he finished reading, he pulled out several pictures and looked at them carefully. He smiled, then put everything back in the envelope and handed it to me.

I went to the table, turned the light on, and started reading. The letter was addressed to the Colonel, written in legible handwriting by the "Commander." He explained the reason he hadn't come for the inspection at 4:00 was because he had never left the Colonel at any time during his life. How about the dream last night? He said he had lied. And indeed, the pictures in the envelope showed him that he was with him, here and there. The inspection had gone fine. He suggested that (1) the Colonel should leave to others the endlessly futile task of improving this Earth; individual well-being depends on the harmonious relationship between one's own perception of the world and others; (2) If one sees the world as a small coin, or a ruined *caravanserai* (roadside inn) that is not even worth a small coin, this person would be the odd one in a majority; (3) Instead of looking for Truth among the people, the individual should return to God, should look inside to find the Divine Mysteries beyond humanity; and (4) The Colonel was decorated with medals of Absence from winning the war of "Self." But he was also reminded that if one tooth outgrows the rest of the teeth in the mouth, the body becomes toothless.

The Colonel passed away in his sleep that night, with or without the help of medication. That we don't know doesn't surprise me. He took that letter as an order.

The letter has been a problem for me ever since it was delivered to our door. Who delivered it? Not the post office, nor any private carrier. The envelope had no sign or stamp. It seemed handwritten and hand-delivered. But who had written it? Who was the Commander? Didn't he have a messenger?

I took the letter and pictures all over, and reactions to them differed. The majority, among them university professors, thought I made it up and simply ignored it. Most religious people considered it heresy. Only a very few accepted it as Gospel without an Apostle.

Questions and Answers about Sainthood and Prophethood

Q: What's the difference between a saint and a prophet?
A: The difference between a saint and a prophet is that a saint has gone through annihilation. All saints have the function of a prophet. However, some prophets have only the function of warning people or dictating orders. This is not the case for true saints.

Q: What is the procedure for being named a saint?
A: In the West, a person must go through many investigations and follow the various canon laws of religious institutions. In the East, saints are named in a more liberal manner. Being named a saint isn't a true test of sainthood.

Q: How can you differentiate a true saint from one who claims to be one or one whom another person or institution claims is one?
A: Their life and their sayings are the main factors. A person who has been annihilated uses a different language and lives a different lifestyle.

Q: Can anyone become a saint?
A: Yes, if they are born with the potential and then go through annihilation. There are no time, geographic, religious, or social restrictions. Anyone who has the potential, who isn't world-hungry, can go through

annihilation and eventually end up in sainthood. Again, annihilation is the most important characteristic. Some prophets have this, some don't. But all true saints do.

Q: Was Mr. Hasan Shushud a saint?
A: Yes.

PART 2

On Itlak, Path of Annihilation

Sayings

Poems

A Story: Hole in the Wall

Questions and Answers about Annihilation

Sayings

〖米〗

Hasan Lutfi Shushud

There are two kinds of journeys: Theoretical and real. One stays on the intellectual level and does not go beyond theories. Their followers pass through the various stages and degrees without experiencing anything.[1]

. . . They devote themselves to books, talks, and interpretation of myths and dreams. The Itlak path is not for readers and talkers. It is for doers.

An aspirant on this road of Itlak doesn't belong to any of the Prophets' religious communities. The Itlak path is not connected to any religious tradition, including ordinary Sufism.[2]

Itlak is not about learning, but about unlearning.

The way of Itlak [*Itlaq Yolu*]:
The real journey is the journey of Annihilation which aims to change perception by:
    Changing of breathing (zikr);
    Changing of eating (fasting);

Going through spiritual suffering (contrition); and
Discussion (fellowship).[3]

This is a hard, long path. But, it guarantees manifestations-
Union-Beyond.[4]

Up to a certain point of this journey is realized by individual
effort, and after that by Divine push.[5]

This journey is beyond faith and beyond heresy.[6] In this journey one will find himself, the Universe, and the Master of
the Universe. This journey is going through consolation to
manifestation.[7]

The way of Itlak [Absolute Liberation] is for those who seek an
escape from the torment of relative reality, the dungeon of existence. They are not satisfied with intellectual, religious attain-
ments. They search for the Absolute Essence. The true nature
of Absence is the source of all religions and esotericism. There
is no way of reaching this source but Annihilation [Fenâ]. It
cannot be attained mentally, intellectually or indirectly.[8]

The most important thing on the Itlak path is while you are
busy with earthly affairs, you silently find the way to wake up
from humanity.[9]

When your hands are busy with work, your heart will be with the
Beloved.

Progress and advancement depend on the individual's persistence and patience and observance of the practices described.[10]

There are many curious about Itlak, but only a few are serious.[11]

The pleasure of Itlak belongs to one who is not religious, but who is longing for the essence of religion.[12]

As they progress through the realm of "being," aspirants will have direct vision of hidden mysteries: Occurrences are seen as non-occurring, events are seen as non-events, and opposites combine, merge.[13]

Itlak Sufism is not pantheism [*tevhid*] nor monism [*vahdeti vücûd*]. It is totally away from "existential systems."[14]

There is no God worshiping on the way of Itlak.[15]

Itlak is not concerned with beatific vision [*cemâl*] reunion, unification [*visal-tevhid*], unity [*ittihad*], etc. The ultimate goal for an Itlak follower is Non-Being, Nothingness, Unseen, Absolute Essence [*ipseity*].[16]

The stages of progress on the way of Itlak:
    Progress towards God;
    Progress in God; and
    Progress beyond God, which is called *baka* [attainment of
        permanent Non-Being]. It is *Ke-en Lem Yekün* [as if it had
        never been experienced] at that stage.[17]

Traversing this path is ascending in perception.[18]

Poems

Mevlana Jalaluddin Rumi

O heart, you go nowhere by talking and gossip.
You cannot reach the Beloved unless
You pass through the door of Absence.
If you do not flutter your wings where His birds fly,
They do not give you arms, wings, O heart.[19]

There is neither question nor answer on the way of
    love,
But only a mystery.
The lover never answers to the religious order.
This is the matter of Absence, not existence.[20]

You have to do something inside of you.
One cannot untie this knot by listening to stories.
One fountain in the house
Is better than a river outside.[21]

The Beloved is coming with a beautiful, sweet smile.
He is so magnificent that he smiles the moon
    and sun.

There is a notion in the world that is spoken to the
    confidants:
"He is everything." He smiles secretly at that
    notion.[22]

Step on the road that has no end to it.
Watching from the distance is not for a man.
Start the journey by the strength of the heart.
Body's strength is for animals.[23]

When Your love touches someone,
Trouble starts pouring immediately on his head.
As soon as Mansür* revealed only a small secret of
    Love,
He was hanged by the rope of envy.[24]

A sage who was advancing on the way to Absence
Passed through the sea of existence like wind.
But, he still had a piece of hair from his existence
That appeared like a zünnâr† in the eyes of
    Absence.[25]

If you start the journey, they will open the road for
    you.
If you annihilate yourself, they will carry you to
    Absence.
Humble yourself, and they will grow you greater than
    the Universe.
Become nothing, and they will show you without
    you.[26]

---

*Hallaj Mansür, a famous Mystic who was killed in 922 because of his beliefs
†A rope girdle formerly worn by early Christians in Turkey

No one can take the ball from Your club.
No one can find You without Your help, just by
    searching.
Though Joseph had the prophetic eyes of Jacob,
Even his nose couldn't get Your smell.*[27]

We are neither impressed by the dome of the sky,
Nor fallen in love with the one whose beauty lasts
    only three days.
You give kindness and sustenance to those who fast,
    O my God!
That's why we have become an ear-ringed slave of
    fasting.[28]

It is customary for Love to eat faith like a meal.
Love neither goes after bread nor the worries of life.
Its table is set beyond day or night.
Then what is fasting?
It is the invitation to a secret feast.[29]

The place where neither I nor space exists,
I ran there following the heart to find soul.
Then I lost my self and time and space.
Neither "this" nor "that" remains with me now.[30]

Take fasting as a basket in your hands.
Let fasting be begging for you on the way of God,
So that God will award you *ab-i hayat*†
And thirst will be satisfied.
Fasting resembles a fragile jar: Don't break it![31]

---

*The legend of the prophets Jacob and Joseph, Koran, Sura 12
†Water of life

Now is the time of patience: The month of fasting
   has come.
For a couple of days, don't talk about a bowl and
   pitchers.
Sit around the table of the sky in order
To free the thread of soul from the cotton ball.[32]

You are the divine light of the sky.
If you were to go faster on the way to God,
You would rise to the sky.
The throne is your place.
Aren't you ashamed of dragging yourself
Like a shadow on the ground?[33]

You will be purified from bad habits by fasting.
You will follow the attained ascent to the sky by
   fasting.
You will be burned like a candle by the fire of
   fasting.
Become divine light. The darkness of a bite makes
   you a morsel for the ground.[34]

The ones who are full with the world are hungry
   for Your Union.
This world's braves tremble in Your separation.
Who looks at a gazelle after seeing Your eyes,
O Beauty, whose hair tied the feet of all lions?[35]

Your Love has left me exhausted.
I have been worn out, ruined on Your path.
I can neither eat during the day, nor sleep at night.
Your Love turned me into my own enemy.[36]

Omar Khayyám

I am suitable for neither the Church nor the Mosque.
With what clay is my tortured body kneaded?
I am like a miserable wretch, an ugly whore.
I have no religion, no world, no hope of heaven.[37]

A Story

Hole in the Wall

Nevit O. Ergin

Once more I walked through the corridors of this old stone building late at night, turning the lights off and closing the doors of every meeting hall in the temple. The sounds of my footsteps were buried in the depths of the thick carpets as my shadow accompanied me silently.

I have done this since early childhood, when my father was alive and the caretaker. He was not the only one: His father, grandfather, and the rest of his ancestors were also the caretakers. The building was once a dungeon for undesirables, then later became an insane asylum. After that it was converted into a school for the highly educated, and finally in the last century it became a Temple of Wisdom for the Wise.

After my father died, I continued the family tradition and took over the duties. I wouldn't know what else I could do. This was an unbreakable caste system. Going out and looking for another job had always scared me. I felt naked and unprotected outside. In the eyes of people, I saw the flash of their predatory instinct, and I thought that unless I became like them, I would remain their prey.

The ones who come to the temple at night try to be caring and loving to each other by replacing their inner instincts with brotherly love. Though I did not see them during the day, at night they practiced. Their rituals are based on the remembrance of a mutual respect and gratitude to the Almighty. They learned to memorize texts from the masters.

Officially I was not allowed to participate in their ceremonies; after all, I was only the caretaker. I would have to be invited and go through serious tests, making vows that I would be one of them. But no one asked me to join. I kept living and working there as a janitor. I loved my job. I respected them and they knew that. Besides, because of my family, I was a part of the building.

The seasons changed outside, but the smell and melancholic darkness of the corridors remained the same. I cleaned the salons and lecture halls during the day. I knew every piece of furniture, lamp, and chandelier, one by one. They related to me the interesting events and conversations of the previous night.

After the evening activities ended, I locked the main gate and retired to my room. This was my prime time. One evening I discovered a small hole in the wall inside my closet. It had been there the whole time, covered by a wooden panel, but I had not noticed it. I took the panel off and saw a small window-sized opening in the wall. I put my head through, but didn't see or hear anything. I found a flashlight, but there was still nothing but darkness. I thought it might have been a ventilation hole between two walls, which was later closed. But there was no wall in front of it. . . .

The next day I asked the engineer who was responsible for the building about it. He also had a set of the building's blueprints. He couldn't find this opening in the blueprints, so I brought him to my room. He was surprised and didn't understand. I asked him if we could make it bigger to see what was behind it. He strongly rejected the idea, saying the wall would collapse and endanger the integrity of the whole floor. I knew he didn't want to be bothered by my silly discovery. He was right, but I couldn't get this small window out of my head. I went back and forth, day and night, trying to find out what was behind there.

As I was, I knew no way I could pass through the small opening. Since I couldn't make the hole bigger, I would have to make myself smaller. I decided to put myself on a strict diet. I didn't eat or drink until sunset, telling those who were curious that I was on a diet.

In the meantime I found a book in the library about fasting. It said fasting would not only change my size, but also my mind. The corporal existence would become spiritual, and the boundaries of time and space would break. It was a small book, written with precise language about life and death, man and God. I read it several times, yet didn't understand most of it. But when I saw the words in the empty space between the lines, my questions disappeared.

After a long period of time with my strict dieting, my size shrunk smaller than the dimensions of the little window. One night after work, when I was alone in the entire building, I decided to explore. I gathered a big flashlight, a rope, and a few other things, and left a note on my table, which read: "Someone once said, 'An unexplored life isn't worth living.'"

It was easy passing through the hole. I was surprised to find myself in one of the small salons. I recognized the bookcases and paintings. It was dark, but dim light and the humming sound of distant conversations were coming from under the doors.

I slowly opened the door. Inside was a dining room smaller than the temple's restaurant. People sat around tables in front of each other, everyone feeding the other. Someone noticed me and showed me the seat next to him. "Welcome, please have a seat," he said. Hesitantly, I did.

There were all kinds of food on the tables, but no utensils. He pretended to give me soup, so I opened my mouth. "Not like that," he said. "You eat with your eyes. This way everyone eats and leaves no mess."

"Thanks, but I can help myself," I replied.

He wondered aloud, "Who is 'Yourself?'"

Instead of getting into that complex question, I answered simply, "I am a caretaker." He didn't understand. "I clean and maintain the building."

"For whom, what building?" he asked.

"For people on the other side of the building," I said.

"I thought he passed away."

I felt cold and uncomfortable. I couldn't even tell this strange person, "Not yet."

Instead I asked feverishly, "Who are you?" I meant to add, "Some kind of zombie?," but I was afraid.

He answered quietly, "You, him, him, him," nodding to the people around his table. "Yes," he said, adding, "and at the same time, none of them."

I was curious and asked, "Where do you live?"

He looked at me as if to ask what kind of question I had just asked. He calmly replied, "Everywhere where everybody lives, not in one particular place."

What was this? People became mirrors of each other. They treated each other well, ate with their eyes, left no mess. There was no predatory instinct. Where was the excitement? I knew life would be boring there, so I excused myself.

"It was nice meeting you, but I have a feeling I don't deserve you and this place. I believe I have some living to do."

"Yes," he said. "'People live at the bottom of Hell and are still afraid of immortality.' That's an old Rumi saying." He added, "Here's one more from him: 'People who live in the dungeon don't even know they carry the key in their hand.'"

I went back the way I had come and passed through the opening of the hole to my room again. At least I was a caretaker. I needed to be needed for living. I locked the door of the closet and put the key in my pocket.

A few weeks have passed since this incident. I've tried not to think about it. I forced myself to forget the hole, and I did not open my closet. I avoided that small salon, but the people I had seen that evening came to my dreams every single night. I was on this side of the building during the days, but I was on the other side at night. Although it was fascinating living a double life in the same body, it was also tiresome.

One day I was called in to meet with the board of directors of the temple. There I was told that my work as a caretaker had been appreciated over the years, but now I should consider retirement. They gave reasons like my age and physical condition.

I was given a pension to cover my basic needs, and two choices. The first was to live in a small apartment, while the second was to go to the temple's retirement home. I was also told they already had a replacement for me. I looked at the faces around the table, and they were all new to me. I asked about the old members and was told they either had died or retired. They said, "When the time comes, it happens to everyone, no exception."

They didn't mention the third alternative. I briefly told my story, and they listened politely. Most of them were bored, though, and thought it was just the nonsense of an old man. At the end I handed them the key to my closet, saying, "Just in case someone wants to go through the hole before they retire."

Questions and Answers about Annihilation

Q: The word "annihilation" has strongly negative connotations. Do you mean the annihilation of our physical body?

A: This annihilation does not refer to the physical body. It's not starvation, nor anorexia. When we talk about annihilation, we mean annihilation of the Self. The Self is our present-day perception. Annihilation is the way of changing that perception to a higher level of perception. On our path, annihilation of Self involves fasting, a different method of breathing called *zikr,* suffering, and some discussion. The path is called the Path of Annihilation.

Q: If you annihilate your Self, how do you survive as a human?

A: Again, it's not physical annihilation. The body is not annihilated. After the Self is annihilated, a higher level of perception is reached, which is called Annihilation of Actions. It is changing human dualistic perception to non-dualistic perception.

Q: Is there a more formal name for this path of annihilation?

A: *Itlaq Yolu* (Itlak). It means the path of liberation. Itlak is merging the opposites. With time and patience, on the Itlak path, all of the intellectual questions—including topics like life and death, God and man—eventually go away. One may not be able to verbalize the answer, but instead realizes that the question has disappeared. That's why we say it's about "unlearning." It's about unlearning everything known.

41

It's not about attending conferences, reading books, or amassing more information. All of that is irrelevant. Itlak is a way to change one's perception. One has to be skeptical and wait until changes in perception are actually experienced.

The tools used on this path to change perception are:

Changing of breathing (zikr);
Changing of eating habits (fasting);
Going through spiritual suffering (contrition); and
Discussion (fellowship).

Discussion is the least important practice. We don't rely on or have any hierarchy or titles, any dress code, any rules or regulations. A guide has very little role in this path. It's not about teaching anyone anything. It's all about an aspirant doing the work themselves—changing their breathing, fasting, and suffering.

Q: How does annihilation of our Being change our perception?
A: Our Being is the result of our present-day perception. We're hooked; we're addicted to this being and becoming business. It's the basis of our life. We cannot slip ourselves out of Being, but eventually, we'll have to. Being and becoming ends when our body dies. If we do consciously stop this process of being and becoming before we die, we call it annihilation: dying before death.

Q: How can the Self be annihilated?
A: By working on the body. The only capital we have is our body. We can use our body as a tool to reach Absence. This is our psychology, our everything. Anything else stays merely at the mental and sensory levels, and that includes all the practices in psychology and all religious dogmas and cult beliefs. To go beyond one's Self, an aspirant has to annihilate themselves. Annihilation is the main thing. Without that, everything is talk. We move from words to ecstasy.

Q: According to Mevlana, "the key to escaping from the dungeon of existence is in our hands." What does that mean?

A: Annihilation is the key. If we were to teach all children and young adults in school about death, we would have a different society than we have now.

Q: So there are stages or levels of Annihilation?

A: Yes. Annihilation of Actions, Annihilation of Attributes, and Annihilation of Essence. It takes time and it happens in stages, spontaneously, like the seasons change. To reach the first stage takes the longest time—eight or ten years, although the time frame varies depending on the individual and their persistence in using the practices—and it's the most challenging stage to reach.

Q: What is the ultimate goal of Itlak?

A: To go beyond the Self. To die before death. To discover something permanent. This life is temporary. We occupy this house for a short period of time. We're going to leave it anyway.

PART 3

On Humankind

Sayings

Poems

A Story: Roxanne

*Questions and Answers about
Humankind*

Sayings

Hasan Lutfi Shushud

Humans are the statues of perception. They represent infinite layers of limited awareness of the totality.[1]

. . . This could be applied to humans, rocks, plants, animals, everything.

We are not the children of Adam, but the children of our perceptions.[2] The Universe is also the shadow of perception.[3]

Human perception represents the level between the realm of Annihilation of Laws [fenâ-i-ahkâm] and Annihilation of Actions [fenâ al-af'âl].[4]

Human perception is the densest degree of perception; objects appear in bodily forms.[5]

In the first degree of Annihilation of Actions, perception changes from the realm of sense perception to the spiritual (potential) world.[6]

Who are we?
A creature by our body;
A Creator by our essence;
Neither creature nor creator by the Essence of our Essence.[7]

You do not know yourself as long as you are with yourself.[8]

Your essence has everything, including the Divinity.[9]

All the power is in your Essence, not with angels nor with God.[10]

Your body is the reflection of a non-being to another non-being.[11]

All, you are; but, "you are" is not You are.[12]

Neither the cosmos nor God exist without you.[13]

Happiness for a human is going beyond humanity.[14]

You are the Beloved, God is your lover, nothing is beyond the Beloved.[15]

Your being is concealed in your non-being; your non-being is concealed in your being.[16]

Man is the shore between infinite being and infinite non-being.[17]

You exist as much as your heedlessness. You suppose the existence of "yourself," "creatures" and "creator."[18]

You are the virgin of Nothingness. You will never have any marriage with the manifestation.[19]

Humanity's greatest skill is blending the opposites.[20]

Your essence is a loan, temporarily given to your body.[21]

You will never know the human until you go beyond the humanity.[22]

Don't envy, don't be jealous of anyone. Their fate is the same: Sorrow, loss, mourning.[23]

You are the essence, He is the secondary.
You are the whole, He is the part.[24]

Mankind has been in a dungeon from birth to death. The strange thing is, they carry the key in their hands.[25]

Poems

Mevlana Jalaluddin Rumi

Fate is not the slave of heart's desire.
Existence is a means to reach Absence.
Our nanny is behind the curtain.
In fact, we are not here; those are our shadows.[26]

You are neither water nor earth; you are something
    else.
You are created from mud, but you are not mud.
You are beyond this muddy world.
You are on the journey to your Essence.
Your body is a riverbed; your soul is the water of life.
But, if you stay with yourself, you won't know either
    one.[27]

I thought I could control my "self's dog"
By putting on the chain of repentance.
Although he is getting tired and old, whenever he
    sees a carcass,
He breaks the chain and attacks.
What can I do with this dog?[28]

O my God, don't leave me in the hands of this
  unreliable self.
Don't make me agree with anyone but You.
I run to you from deceits, troubles from my self.
I am Yours. Don't give my self back to me.[29]

You are the copy of the Divine book.
You are the mirror of the Sultan's art, beauty and
  power.
Everything in the Universe is not beyond you.
Whatever you want, ask from you,
Whatever you look for, search for in you.[30]

It is amazing that the Beloved is contained in my
  heart.
Souls of thousands of bodies fit in this flesh.
One grain grows into thousands of harvests.
Hundreds of universes fit in the eye of a needle.[31]

O one who enjoys the tunes of doubt and
  suspicion,
All these are your imagination coming from your
  confused heart.
You are "Nothing" and "Nothing" cannot be
  displayed to your eyes
As a "something" better than this.[32]

A human who hasn't gone beyond himself
Has not become man yet.[33]

You are the Divine Light, the light of the sky.
If you go faster on the way to God,
You will rise to the sky. The throne is your place.

Aren't you ashamed of dragging yourself like a
    shadow on the ground?[34]

Why does this night-blind sorrow grab my neck and
    not let go?
I wonder, who is blind, that sorrow or me?
I am in the sky; this clay body of mine is my
    reflection.
Who could steal a star from the water?[35]

A human is made by mixing opposite materials.
His shape is drawn on the table of sorrow; his clay is
    carved by grief.
Sometimes he is an angel, sometimes a devil, and
    sometimes a beast.
How could those qualities mix together?[36]

Night has come; it's time for people to fall asleep,
Like the fish that plunges back into water.
In the morning, most will follow the steps of reason.
Only a few will walk towards the One who created
    reason.[37]

Some people tell stories about the Beyond.
Some expect help from the Beyond.
Souls keep running out of bodies secretly
Looking for the Beyond.[38]

One who has boarded a sailing boat
Sees that trees are moving on the shore.
It is like that: We are passing by through the world,
But we think that the world is passing us.[39]

They brought us here from the tavern of *Elest**
As drunks, as exuberants.
We came from Absence to Existence.
They will pull us back again to that tavern.[40]

Look at your body as a whole:
A bunch of drunks, fallen upon each other, sleeping.
If you want them to become friends of yours,
Yell to them: "Wake up!"
And then don't go away after you've awoken these
    sleepers.[41]

When your heart is cleansed from your being,
You will see yourself reflected in the Beloved.
It is impossible to see your face without a mirror.
Look at the Beloved: His face is your mirror.[42]

O moon-faced Beloved, if you are in love with our
    Love,
Free yourself from the bondage of six dimensions.
If you are looking for that Love, move into the sea of
    heart.
Why do you stop at the edge of the river?[43]

Leave to others that endless job of the improvement
    of this earth,
Because the whole world isn't worth a piece of barley
Or a ruined *caravanserai*.†
It isn't worth even a small coin.[44]

---

*"Am I not your God?" Koran VII, 171–73
†A roadside inn where travelers rest and recover from the day's journey

You are in my eyes. If not, how could I see You?
You are in my mind. If not, how could I be an insane
    lover?
There is a place, I don't know where.
If Your Love isn't there, how could I be there?[45]

I am not me, you are not you, you are not me.
Also, I am me, You are You, and You are me.
O beauty of *Hotan*,* I am so confused with you
That I am not sure—am I you, or are you me?[46]

---

*A city in western China, just east of Pakistan

A Story

Roxanne

Nevit O. Ergin

She carefully counted all the money I gave her and said, "Where is the rest? You're five hundred dollars short."

I looked at her face. There was neither beauty nor mercy there. Instead I saw the pleasure of a predator in her eyes. "Mrs. Hunter," I said, attempting to appeal to her generosity, "this is all I have."

"I have my principles never to compromise with a tenant," she replied.

Mrs. Hunter was my landlord—a round, middle-aged, matronly lady with one arm. She always tilted her shoulder to her amputated arm's side. Although I was curious, I never dared ask about her missing arm.

I was two months behind in rent. When I gave her the rent now, she demanded that I also add a five-hundred-dollar security payment. I realized she was determined. "Give me a little time," I begged.

"Here," she said, "this is your eviction notice. If I don't have the money by 5:00 p.m., the locks will be changed and your belongings will be out."

When she left, I was shaking. I looked around. This was the house I had lived in for most of my life. It had become another body for me. The geometry of every space was carved into my mind and existence. I could walk through the rooms and hallways in the dark without any problems.

It was not only me; the whole community lived here. Any time I got a little money, I bought exotic plants like quince and pomegranate trees, different types of jasmine and honeysuckle, and even a couple of grape trunks. I had made a small pond and put goldfish in it, and my little backyard had turned into a paradise. I bribed the neighborhood birds with fancy seeds. Blue jays and cardinals came with their cheerful songs and became permanent residents of the garden.

Guests used to say, "Why are you spending so much money? You are just a tenant."

But my father always told me, "Son, be a tenant in this world. If someone tells you whose tenant you are, kiss his hand."

I knew he was right. Since we are all temporary in this world, we shouldn't get attached to anything.

That's why I didn't consider buying the house, even when I *had* money.

But now I was forced to say good-bye to everyone, hoping that whoever came after me would take care of them. And when I went outside I realized how easily one could become homeless. I felt uneasy and scared. All the comforts and security that a home provided were gone. A sense of urgency was clouding my thinking process. I had a couple of hours to find five hundred dollars.

I didn't have the talent or labor skills worth that kind of money. My basic source of income was my social security check, which came at the beginning of each month. I had used that already to cover the rent. That left me with one last chance: to borrow from friends and relatives.

I don't have many friends or relatives, though. The only friend I have is a poor, homeless fellow who I'm sure will just say, "You can come join me." The only relative I have is my rich younger brother who would give me a long lecture about my age, saying I should move into a nursing home. *No wonder the rich become rich,* I thought to myself. *It's because of their greed. And the poor stay poor because they are generous.*

I was walking on a narrow street, which ended at a small park on the shore. I felt I was being followed by someone. I turned around and saw it was a small black dog that I hadn't even paid attention to. I increased my pace, but the dog did the same.

I stopped and turned back suddenly. The dog stopped too. We looked at each other. It was a darling. I said, "Look, I don't know what you want from me, but it's not a good time. I'm not sure if I have a place to stay, but I know for sure that I don't need a dog right now. Get lost."

I have no idea if it understood my frustration from the tone of my voice, but its tiny yellow eyes were full of joy behind the long black hairs on its face. Its wet tongue was sticking out as it shook its head.

I started walking fast again. After about a hundred yards I stopped and looked back at the dog, still sitting in the same place. I turned on the next corner and then the next, doing everything I could so the dog could not find me. I felt relieved getting rid of this nuisance.

It was 3:00 in the afternoon. I remembered I had two hours left to find my money. I had already given up, though. Total submission took over my sorrow and hopelessness. I walked toward the park, but then suddenly realized the dog was still after me. I slowed down, and it passed me, continuing on to the park.

This time I followed the dog. I sat on the bench and it came to sit in front of me. I wasn't paying much attention; the park was empty. When I went to use the restroom, I noticed a small bulletin board on the wall. Among all kinds of community news and adver-tisements, a photocopied photo caught my attention. It read, "My name is Roxanne, have you seen me?" There was a picture of a small black dog, and written underneath were the words: "Reward—five hundred dollars." A telephone number was at the bottom. I didn't go to the toilet, instead I left. The dog was sitting in the same spot when I yelled, "Roxanne, Roxanne!"

Then the little dog ran to me.

Questions and Answers
about Humankind

Q: How do you define Essence?

A: Essence is Truth. Where Truth begins and ends is unknown. The Truth is our Essence. In other words, man is a stage of this Essence. There are unlimited layers of perceptions, each with a limited awareness of the Essence. Essence is the Truth, or Truth itself. The cosmos, time, space, God, creatures, every element of life, are a result of our human perception. During the stages of annihilation, one becomes more and more aware about the Essence. Then Truth and Essence become the same.

Q: Does Itlak help you change your habits and behaviors?

A: By changing our perception we deal with our Essence rather than our shadow. Our behavior is the shadow of our Essence. Unless we move our hand, the shadow of our hand won't change. Through annihilation we change our perception. We stay in our Essence, but on a different perceptional level.

Q: Is the Self the same thing as Being?

A: Being is the shadow of our origin, the shadow of our Essence. In other words, being and becoming are all about our existence in this world. Our human perception creates us as separate from the whole, and that's where the trouble starts. Our being and becoming always bothers us, even if we're not conscious about it.

Q: But then how can you say, "When you take one step toward God, God is taking ten steps toward you?"

A: A better way to say that might be, "your Essence." Your Essence is beyond God. "When you take one step toward your Essence, your Essence is taking ten steps toward you."

Q: Why is it necessary for Essence to be incarnated in life?

A: That's the question of questions. There are theories. One theory is that God was beautiful and He wanted to be seen, so He created the universe. I suppose any speculation is as good as any other, but I don't believe any of them.

PART 4

On God

Sayings

Poems

A Story: Garden of Eden

Questions and Answers about God

Sayings

Hasan Lutfi Shushud

God is the Unmanifested element in the dualist system that is produced by our ordinary human perception, the origin and destination of the created Universe. In this duality, the Manifested elements are the created world, all the creatures including humanity. The Unmanifested is the Creator (God).[1]

God is your Essence, not your creator.[2]

God is the Absence of every being.[3]

So many people talk about God, but nobody knows Him.[4]

The Creator is not aware about the creatures.[5]

A person's love for God is a metaphor. Unless someone thinks God is a person, how can someone love an unknown God?[6]

Look for God, who assembles everything and at the same time is exempt from everything.[7]

Poems

Mevlana Jalaluddin Rumi

If you are a believer, He is searching for you.
If you are a disbeliever, He is calling you.
Walk this way, become faithful, go there, become
    unfaithful.
Both are the same for Him.[8]

What are you looking for in the land of illusion?
Why are you washing your eyes with the blood of
    your heart?
All your being, head to toe, is God.
O ignorant one who doesn't know Himself,
What are you looking for besides You?[9]

You are such a being that
He is your existence, He is your Absence.
He is the source of your joy and sorrow.
You don't have the eyes to see Him.
You are Him, head to toe.[10]

There is Someone who is neither up nor down,
That is precious either with or without us.
Don't say, "He is here, He is there."
The whole Universe is full of Him,
But where is He?[11]

You said, "Tell," but words can't reveal that secret.
Never mind my tongue. Nothing in the whole
        Universe could tell it.
It is impossible to talk about the breath
That was mixed with the dust of Adam.*[12]

O heart, if you are aware of these words,
"God is with you wherever you are,"†
Why are you so confused?
But if you forget this,
You attribute a partner to God.[13]

Your body is not kneaded by clay.
God did lots of favors when creating you.
You are yelling, calling Him,
He is answering: "Come in."[14]

You have two hands, two feet, two eyes. That is
        true.
But it is a mistake to count heart and the Beloved
        as two.
It is only a pretext saying, "Beloved."
In fact, God is the Beloved.
Whoever says God is two is impious, an infidel.[15]

---

*"I designed Adam, blew into him from my spirit." Koran: 38–72
†He is with you wherever you are. Koran 57–4

The Union with God cannot be achieved
Until a person completely annihilates his Self.
Such a Union is not the merging of two to make one.
Union is your total annihilation.
Absurdity doesn't turn falsehood into truth.
Only a fool says, "Everything is God."[16]

They will not allow you to go inside of yourself
While you keep staying with your Self.
Only if you annihilate the Self will they keep you
    in their eyes and hearts.
Only if you give up both worlds will they stamp
    you with the seal of Absence.[17]

He is in the meaning, not in the words.
He is in the heart, not on the tongue.
He is the Essence of the Universe, but not the
    Universe.
He is neither in Absence nor Existence.[18]

The world is charmed by His attributes.
Everything, everyone seems to exist.
But, they are annihilated in front of Him,
And only the one who can lift the curtain of
    mortality
May reach His Essence behind His attributes.[19]

O One who ties our hands with tales, deceits,
Don't pull the skirt of Union from Love's drunks.
You are such a prey that freed Yourself from the
    trap of heart's worshippers.
I would be an infidel if I said You exist among the
    existing ones.[20]

You make me drunk at the place of worship.
You let me stay at *Kaaba,** but make me pray to
   idols.
I don't understand either Your goodness or Your
   badness.
Use me for whatever You want. I am in Your hands. [21]

*A shrine faced by Muslims when praying

A Story

Garden of Eden

Nevit O. Ergin

Billy," she said, "this is my friend."

I was introduced to a hummingbird. Despite its customary rush, the hummingbird hesitated and managed to smile. "Hi," it said and then flew away.

"Old friend, it's been at least ten years since we've seen each other," I added. But it was forty years ago when I had met her overseas at a mutual friend's house. She was a beautiful teenager, but throughout the years she had kept her charm and beauty. Now she was a beautiful sixty-some-year-old lady.

We had morning coffee in her backyard, looking out at the small garden. The coffee had a pleasant vanilla aroma. My chair was already covered in the morning sun. "It's going to be eighty again," she said as she looked to the sky dotted with a few high-sitting white clouds and a low-lying strip of the city's fog.

The small house was clustered with other small houses on a hill around a big metropolitan city. But the backyard was ingeniously designed with fences covered with morning glories and star jasmines hiding the neighbors' houses. A few trees were smartly planted to give the yard the perception of depth.

She knew every inch of this garden. Jose, the elderly gardener, was like smoke blending between the lawn and plants. He came early Wednesday mornings, mostly bending over plants, never talking unless spoken to. With his hat and sweater, he became part of the landscape on hot summer days.

I noticed two cats sleeping in the shade. One was in one corner, the other was opposite. She introduced the cats casually: The black cat was Slicker and the calico was Edith. But I sensed an attachment in her voice. She was burning to talk about them. "How come they stay so far apart from each other?" I asked.

"I wish Jones was alive," she responded.

Jones was the third cat. He was more mature, and the intermediary between Slicker and Edith. Months ago, in the middle of the night, Jones was mauled by a coyote and died in the front yard. The relationship between Slicker and Edith was never the same after that.

Slicker comes home and goes to bed at midnight and wants to have his breakfast at six in the morning. God knows where he usually spends his days and nights. It was surprising that he was sleeping in the yard. After losing Jones, Edith became the opposite of Slicker. She became very social, staying around and wanting all the attention.

In the meantime, I was introduced to a yellow butterfly. It asked where I was from. A few bumblebees came to check my smell. The hornet was not welcomed by my friend. But the real show was the power line in front of us where a dozen well-fed black pigeons had taken their places, some facing us and some facing the city. They were all talking among themselves. Every so often one would get the urge to fly, and the rest of them would flutter their wings and follow it. It didn't take long before they were back taking their seats on the power line.

A question came to my mind, "Where were these pigeons' nests?" We looked around, but they weren't around. I pointed to Jose with my head. My friend asked Señor Jose, "May I ask a question?"

He stood up and turned to us.

"Where are the pigeons' homes?"

He looked at the pigeons, and without searching for a nest said, "In your heart, Señora, in your heart."

I was amazed at how quickly Señor Jose had found the right place for the pigeons.

Billy came again and brought a bunch of other hummingbirds. I knew he was showing me to his friends.

When the sun started to burn, my friend sprinkled water around and then we went inside. Mr. Jose kept working.

On these long summer days, the next chance to go outside was around 7:00 p.m.

Two steps down, a table was set for us with a bottle of wine, fresh vegetables, and a pale citronella lantern burning slowly. I had an exciting experience on one of my steps, when one of my feet didn't land sufficiently, and I kissed the ground. A hawk saw that and screamed, "Be careful, Baba."

This small yard had everything the Garden of Eden had. We felt no need to leave home except to make a short trip for groceries. Days and nights followed each other till that day.

I was sipping the coffee with the vanilla fragrance. The sun was pleasantly warm. Tomatoes were ripening in the small vegetable patch, roses were in bloom, and the morning glories were smiling.

Then I noticed that no hummingbirds were around. No butterflies. No bees. Jose hadn't shown up either. My friend noticed the same thing.

"No pigeons either," she remarked. Our eyes were fixed on the power line.

"Maybe it's too early," I said.

"But they used to wake up much earlier," she answered.

"Strange . . . " Suddenly I felt a cool breeze of loneliness come over me.

"Let's wait," she suggested.

It didn't take long before about a dozen strange birds began to appear in the sky. They were all alike, but there was something strange about them. They didn't have any feathers; they resembled naked chickens.

We were wondering about the origin of these birds when we heard the neighbor calling from behind the fence. He was invisible since the fence was covered in green. My friend approached the neighbor's voice.

He was excited. "Did you see the birds?" he asked. "They were all bioengineered, some DNA from a chicken, some from a falcon. It took scientists a long time. They resist diseases and they taste better than chicken."

My friend asked, "What about the hummingbirds, butterflies, and bees?"

The neighbor summed it all up. "Environmental pollution. Another nice thing about these birds is that they clean everything up."

Then she remembered Jose and asked about him.

"He was undocumented," the neighbor quietly answered.

Questions and Answers
about God

Q: Do you worship God in Itlak?
A: There is no God-worshiping in Itlak.

Q: If someone has a particular belief about God, do they have to give it up to follow the Itlak path?
A: No. We're not about to interfere with anyone's religion or religious beliefs. Mind, reason, and faith are all clothes custom-made by and worn by humans. At a certain point in time, we usually outgrow and alter them. Our perceptions naturally change throughout our lifetime. Our idea of God changes, just like our idea of everything else changes. Itlak is about changing our perception to a higher level of perception. An aspirant doesn't have to give up anything. They just have to fast and do zikr—which will bring suffering—and wait. Their perception changes slowly and naturally.

Q: Do you believe in God's will in our lives?
A: God has nothing to do with us. In other words, if we believe in God or not, God doesn't care. If we take our journey on a speedy horse or a lame donkey, for God it's the same. This will hurt a lot of people's dreams, but this is it. They all say they love God and pray to God so He will give a little preference, a little privilege in this world and the next world. But, there is no such thing.

Q: Does God even exist?

A: In the human perception, which is one layer out of an infinite number of layers of perceptions, we see ourselves as created by a creator. Likewise, the whole universe, including all its creatures, is created by this creator. That necessitates the creation of God. The whole thing is a result of our human dualistic perception. In that perception, we have a perceiver, we have a perceived. We think these are two different things. The perceiver sees a physically existing universe. Actually, if one goes above this level of perception to non-dualistic perception, they will see that the perceiver and perceived are the same. They will see that our Essence is far beyond God. We are the Beloved; God is the lover.

Q: Does praying to God, then, do any good?

A: Only to sooth the pain in suffering (contrition). God doesn't care if someone prays or not. If praying makes someone feel good, they should pray.

Q: How can you question the belief of someone who sincerely loves God?

A: How can a person love the unknown? Everyone says "I love God." We hear that all the time. This is a metaphor. Actually, a person cannot love God.

Q: Would you summarize how Itlak describes God, the universe, and our role in it?

A: Our human perception is one of an unlimited number of layers of perception. We don't know how animals see the world, how plants see it, how molecules see it, but we believe that all creatures have perception. We believe that we're the result of perhaps a billion, a trillion years of the evolution of perception. And, perception goes on and on with unlimited layers above and below our human level. What we represent humbly is just one glimpse of this awareness of the Truth, of our Essence.

In our life, we find ourselves and others and the universe. We imagine that God made it, "others," and "me" as well. Preferences between "me" and "others" are the cause of all the predatory actions in this world. In other words, when I see myself and others, I prefer myself to them. I naturally take advantage of others. I become the predator, while the "others" become the prey. The only exception to this is with motherhood, whether in humans or animal: For a brief period of time, the offspring and the mother have an unselfish relationship. As long as our human situation stays like this, there will be no peace on the Earth. This conflict becomes infinite.

In any case, all these creatures need one creator. This need eventually leads to the creation of God. In other words, God did not create me; I created God. On this faulty perception, we have duality: God and the rest of us. This is the human dualistic perception. When one separates themselves from God in this duality, they have to create the devil also. One has to be born. One has to die.

We're trying to get out from this existential suffering by annihilation. We think we're caged, we're in a dungeon, and the key in our hand is annihilation. We have to free ourselves from our Self which created all this mess so we don't die, so we reach Absence, non-being, Nothingness.

Q: Is the devil something created by our human perception, too?
A: Anyone who says, "The devil made me do it," or anything similar, coming from religion or anywhere else, is giving a partner to God, which again, is a result of our human, dualistic perception.

Q: Does that mean Creation never happened?
A: Exactly. We were never born. The universe has never been created. This is a key concept.

But, if we consider that all our troubles start with our Existence, our Being, then we can settle this issue through annihilation of Self, annihilation of Being. We accept Self, then there are others and, of course, then there is the universe. Most people believe these are pre-existing conditions. In fact, we were born at the top of that. We find ourselves in this world as if it already existed. There is no such thing. It's very important to understand this. We're the silkworm. The universe is our cocoon. This cocoon doesn't exist before the silkworm, the silkworm makes the cocoon out of its saliva. In other words, we bring our universe. We bring the others. They did not exist before us. We brought them. This is the product of our perception. Our brain creates them. This is why science can't go too far. It's just like a dog trying to catch its tail.

Q: Why can't we experience that within our human perception?
A: Well, again, the characteristic of this perception doesn't allow us to experience anything like that. There is no blame involved. It's just the level where we stand.

PART 5

On Religion

Sayings

Poems

A Story: Prey for Serenity

Questions and Answers about Religion

Sayings

Hasan Lutfi Shushud

An aspirant on this road of Itlak doesn't belong to any of the Prophets' religious communities.[1]

Religion is rules and regulations designed to ensure human happiness in this world and after.[2]

If all divine scriptures came from the Absolute Truth, why all these multiple religions?[3]

Oh my God, there are so many tales on the heart and tongue about your majesty.[4]

When we pray, our humanity prays for our essence, not to any divine plane.[5]

Religion came from Mysticism, not otherwise.[6]

Religions are conceived by humans.[7]

If the truths came forward, the history of religion would become upside down.[8]

Religion has brought to people more trouble than benefit.[9]

The ones who couldn't find the Truth created ceremonies and religions.[10]

Religion came for our earthly happiness, but did not succeed. Human intelligences are about to destroy each other.[11]

Poems

Mevlana Jalaluddin Rumi

Not before the minarets and mosques come down
Will the *Kalenderi's** affairs be settled.
Not before faith becomes heresy and heresy becomes
    faith
Will anyone become a Muslim.[12]

Know this very well: A Lover cannot be a Muslim.
In the religion of Love, there is neither faith nor
    blasphemy;
Neither body nor soul; neither reason nor heart.
Whoever is not like that, he is not a Lover.[13]

On the way of Union, neither worship nor sin
    counts.
Who is a pauper and who is a sultan in this tavern?
It doesn't matter if a Kalenderi's face is white or black.
What is the brightness of the sun or the moon before
    the Throne of God?[14]

---

*A *Kalenderi* is a kind of Sufi, a dervish who has renounced the world and denounced
Self by shaving his hair, subjecting himself to humiliation.

A Story

Prey for Serenity

Nevit O. Ergin

I thought I would be the first at the park to watch the sunrise, but there was a lady dressed in a black jumpsuit standing on the edge of the water. She was facing the horizon where the sun was about to rise. Her bag was on the bench I used to sit on every morning.

Naturally I was disappointed and sat on the next bench. I started to watch her strange dancing. I am sure there is a more proper name for the slow, harmonious movements of arms, hands, and legs that she was making. I am also sure every move had a deep meaning and explanation. But I wasn't going to ask about these from the lady who was so deeply involved in her motions. I was sorry that I knew so little about this exotic dance that had been practiced by millions for centuries.

Looking at her, I sensed an invisible wall hiding her from the rest of the world. The scarf that covered her hair was also covering a part of her face, giving her an obscure serenity.

Her movements changed; they became stranger and faster with the rising sun on the horizon. Then she stopped.

She returned to the bench. I didn't know if she was aware of my existence. I turned my head to the other side and stayed still. But I was curious, and when I looked at her again, she was meditating. Her feet were crossed under her legs, and her arms were stretched with her hands resting on her knees. Her eyes were closed.

I was afraid to disturb her silence. I got up and walked toward the other bench farther away, behind the bushes. There I could see her between the branches, but she couldn't see me.

I noticed a couple of ducks showed up out of nowhere, with more following them. Some had green feathering on their neck. They all walked aimlessly with a great sway. She acted like she didn't notice them, staying motionless in the lotus position. I was praying these nuisances wouldn't destroy her meditation.

Then she suddenly jumped off the bench with remarkable speed and grabbed one of the ducks by the neck. She squeezed hard, and I could barely hear the weak, desperate sound of the duck. The rest of the birds ran off, some even tried to fly.

This crime scene was so short and quick that no one seemed even to notice. The lady put the lifeless duck in a bag and walked away.

Questions and Answers about Religion

Q: How does Itlak differ from pantheism, monism, and "existential systems?"

A: They all consider the world as physically existing before us. We, on the other hand, don't believe creation ever took place. There is no existence besides us. So if one doesn't believe in existence, how can this existence be modified, unified? Pantheism is taking the world too seriously, as if something really, really exists.

Lots of people believe there's a perceiver and a perceived. In Itlak, we change from this dualistic perception to a non-dualistic perception. In a non-dualistic perception, the perceiver and perceived become the same; God and creatures become the same; good and bad become the same; death and life become the same; Lover and Beloved become the same. Itlak fuses all of the opposites. The point is reached where all we see is nothing but potential. It's the first thing we realize. I know this table is really a table, but I reach the point where, when I touch it, I feel like I'm dreaming it, that I've made it up. It could be or not be.

Q: But God, or many Gods, is the center of most religions.

A: In the earthly way, religion comes between man and God. If someone becomes religious, they're on the side of God. If they're not, they're on the side of the devil. Everyone who goes to war goes in the name of God. Both sides claim He is on their side. That is their perception. More people have been killed in the name of God than of anything else.

Q: Is any one religion better than others?
A: No. Truth is at the root of all religions, but what have religions done with the Truth? All the religions give their own versions of the Truth. Absolute Truth cannot be in multiples.

Q: How is Itlak related to Sufism?
A: Itlak is a Sufi tradition. However, it has no religious affiliation and no God worshiping. It is not the Islamic Sufism that is generally described and currently practiced. If we were to say that Itlak is the essence of Islam, that would be true, but it would be equally true to say it is the essence of all religions, the essence of everything.

Meeting with Hasan Shushud

>•◄

Millicent Alexander

Millicent Alexander has been on the Itlak path since 1972.

It was June of 1972 and I was twenty-four years old. I had committed myself financially, intellectually, and emotionally to attending a spiritual school in Sherborne, England, the following fall. The school was run by a man named J. G. Bennett.

Most of my friends were going to attend the same school, including my college boyfriend, whom I had just broken up with—possibly prematurely. They were going to show up later in the year; I was the only one of my friends who had a teaching job and who therefore was ready to take off in June. I was also the only one suffering from a young broken heart, aching to get away as soon as possible. Off to Europe solo it was then. My goal: Become enlightened.

I had joined a Gurdjieff group in San Francisco in 1970, right after graduating from the University of California, Berkeley, and getting my first teaching job. Gurdjieff was a spiritual teacher from Armenia who died in 1949. I had been introduced to him by my college boyfriend, who had been reading about Gurdjieff and his work in P. D. Ouspensky's *In Search of the Miraculous*.

After my first year with the San Francisco group, the two group leaders—a husband and wife—took off to India in search of their own spiritual teacher. After making connections in India, they had broken their ties with Gurdjieff's teachings and relocated to a spiritual center only a few miles from Bennett's Sherborne. The husband wrote to all of us group members, suggesting that if we wanted to continue our spiritual studies in the tradition of Gurdjieff, we should study with J. G. Bennett in England. Most of us took him up on his suggestion. All of us who applied were accepted.

The couple invited me to stay with them for the first week or so that I was in Europe. I had contacted Bennett to let him know I was arriving early, and he, in turn, had agreed to meet with me to confirm my acceptance to his school.

I was excited and also a bit terrified to meet Bennett. He was something of a legend with the members of our group, famous for saying and doing unexpected things. What if he told me he'd changed his mind about my acceptance at his school?

When I arrived at Sherborne House for the interview, the fortress-like building was waiting, just like in the photos. An imposing three stories, with the promise of old, cold, damp, empty English rooms, which somehow seemed oddly inviting.

I walked through the heavy wooden door to be greeted by a trim, middle-aged woman who ushered me into Bennett's office. He was sitting in a wooden swivel chair facing a large desk. What a big man! His black suit made him look even bigger, and I couldn't help noticing how much wild, white hair he had. He looked up and motioned me to sit down in a chair to the left of his desk.

"So, you're coming to Sherborne next year."

"Yes."

"And you know the school is closed now. You know you're here early. You know the others won't arrive until October."

"Yes. I have three months to travel. Is there any place in particular you think I should go?"

Bennett was quiet. After a few minutes, he pulled out a piece of paper and pen from a desk drawer, wrote a note, slipped it in an envelope, addressed the envelope to Bey Hasan Shushud, 27 Beyaz Karenfil Sok., III Levent, Turkey, then offered it to me.

"Yes. I'd like you to go to Turkey to meet a friend of mine. His name is Bey Hasan Shushud. You must go by land—don't fly. Give him this note. I've written out his address for you. Good luck. We'll see you in October."

I took the note, thanked him with a little bow, then left. Hmmm. It hadn't seemed anything like what one would call an interview. On the other hand, I was still invited to attend his school, and now I had a goal for the summer—get to Turkey. What would this friend be like?

A few days later, I boarded a train to Paris where I boarded the Orient Express, which took me through Italy to what was then Yugoslavia, to the city of Zagreb. I switched to a train headed for Split, took a boat to Dubrovnik, reboarded the train to Beograd, and finally landed in Istanbul.

After settling into the American Hotel in Istanbul, I took a taxi to III Levent and knocked on the door at 27 Beyaz Karenfil Sokak, a simple two-story, middle-class home in a neighborhood of Istanbul on the European side of the city.

A woman opened the door. She looked like she was in her 60s; hair medium-length with streaks of gray and a bit frizzy. She was plump around the middle like a grandmother, with skinny legs, dressed in Western skirt and blouse. Later, I found out her name was Nuriye Hanim, and she was Mr. Shushud's wife. I handed her the note given to me by Bennett. She asked me to wait, disappeared, and a few minutes later, Mr. Shushud appeared at the door.

He was a small man, thin, a bit fragile-looking if you just gave him a quick glance. He was balding with a rim of gray hair and thick, bushy eyebrows and dressed in dark brown pants; a white long-sleeved shirt, perfectly pressed; and a skinny black tie. His black tie-shoes were polished. At the time, he was seventy-two years old. He didn't look at me, but rather offered me his hand as he opened the door wider to allow my entry.

"Welcome, my child. Please come in."

Mr. Shushud ushered me into the living room. The walls were covered with framed works of calligraphy, black on parchment, and the floors and furniture were covered with rugs and kilims, mostly burgundies with traditional Persian designs. All of his many books were covered in gold paper.

He gestured that I should sit on one end of a sofa with carved wooden legs and arms covered with some kilims, actually more of a settee. He sat on an armless chair next to it, a chair that looked like it could have been from an early twentieth-century formal parlor. His wife brought us cookies and strong Turkish tea in small glasses that tinkled on their saucers. I don't remember much of that first conversation. I'm sure he asked me how I got to Turkey and where I was staying, and no doubt he asked about Mr. Bennett's health.

This I wrote in my journal: *He asked me what my plans were for the following year.*

"I'm going to study with Mr. Bennett in England next year."

"But, my child, you have to protect your health, and it's so cold in England."

I didn't have time to sort out the meaning of his last sentence, which is why I later wrote it down. He immediately continued to say that while I was in Turkey it would be too dangerous for me to stay at the hotel for Americans. I was to stay at his house with him and his wife.

One kind word led to another, and he finally suggested that I go back to my hotel, get my things, and return the next morning. He and Nuriye Hanim walked me to the door. Looking down and away, he shook my hand good-bye, reminding me again to take care.

I appeared on his doorstep the next day with my North Face backpack swinging from my shoulders.

He showed me the room where I would be staying, upstairs and in the back. It was his son's room, his son whom he indicated was in London. The room was smallish with a shaded window, a bed, and a dresser. The walls were bare, with one exception: Some curious brown gift-wrap paper, covered with a design of car wheels, had been taped to the wall next to the bed.

After I got settled in, Mr. Shushud invited me to join him in the

Millicent Alexander, Nuriye Hanim, and Hasan Shushud in 1972,
Istanbul, Turkey

living room. He spoke mostly in English, but sometimes in French, both fluently. He and Nuriye Hanim spoke together in Turkish.

Nuriye Hanim was clearly a good cook and housekeeper and devoted to Mr. Shushud. She served us breakfast, lunch, or tea as the day required, but she never ate with us. During meals, we didn't speak much. We ate lunch in the dining room and breakfast on trays in the living room, always sitting in the same spot as during our first conversation. Tea, on the other hand, was full of conversation.

Mr. Shushud gave little information about his own life, and the questions he asked me about mine revolved around my plans for my future. He had already started with a persistent theme—reminding me how cold it was in England and how important it was to take care of my health.

He referred to a friend whom he had known for many years, a doctor, a wonder man who lived in America, in Detroit. Perhaps I would meet him. This doctor friend always visited Mr. Shushud, "time by time." Mr. Shushud didn't give any specific time references, but at some point "many years ago," he had given this doctor a rose to insert in the front of a collection of poems by Mevlana Jalaluddin Rumi. This collection was named *Güldeste,* which means "rose" in Turkish. I had never heard of Mevlana.

He responded by telling me that one day I must read the poetry of Mevlana. Had I heard of the whirling dervishes? I had not. He often spoke of Mevlana during our subsequent conversations, and sometimes when he did, tears would slide softly down his cheeks.

He explained that Mevlana speaks often of fasting as a good way to make spiritual progress. He didn't explain a particular method of fasting, nor did he suggest that I should start the practice.

I asked him how long he thought I should stay in Turkey, because I needed to purchase a ticket back to English. "You must learn patience, my child," was all he said. I was to hear him repeat those exact same six words almost daily throughout my three weeks in Istanbul.

The next morning at breakfast, Mr. Shushud broke what was to me the bad news. He told me he had some friends across the street who had invited me to stay with them. Then, in response to my silence, he urged me not to be disappointed, because they would make excellent accommodations for me, and I would return to stay in his son's room in a few days. He expressed his concern that it was too crowded at his house and therefore "inconvenient" for me.

He invited me to come for breakfast and tea every day, because, according to him, we had so much to talk about.

I don't remember the names of any of the other people I met in Turkey, including this family. The father and two daughters were fluent in English; the mother spoke only Turkish. They gave me a huge room in the front of the house and treated me like I was royalty. I was an American, but more important, I was a guest of Mr. Shushud.

That first night that I slept across the street it was screechingly hot. Because of this, I had left all my bedroom windows open during dinner—and forgot to turn off the lights. When I came up for bed, the room was filled with mosquitoes. Mosquitoes eat me alive and I have a phobia about them—the whirring they make when they're close to my ear is worse than a dentist's drill. Plus, after they bite me, the bites swell and turn bright red, and it's only a matter of time until I scratch them until they bleed. Naturally, I get covered with scabs and scars and plenty of itching.

To avoid this desperate scenario, I spent the next hour killing them by slapping a magazine against the walls wherever they had landed. I felt a little guilty about keeping everyone in the family awake, but no one came to my room to ask about the racket, to ask what the crazy American was doing. (I found out later as I was getting ready to leave Turkey that they had had to wash all of the walls to get the squashed mosquitoes off.)

The next day was breakfast with Mr. Shushud as he had promised.

He asked me how I had slept. I complained that my room was filled with mosquitoes and that it took about an hour to kill them all. I explained how mosquitoes and their bites make me crazy.

He advised that I should be grateful for every mosquito bite that I ever had or would get. By way of explanation, he said that if someone is on God's road, they will get plenty of mosquito bites, but they will be protected from "the total disasters."

It was during this breakfast that he introduced me to Itlak Yolu, saying only that it teaches the importance of fasting and a way of breathing called zikr, and "the evergreen suffering."

He asked again about California. He had heard that it was always very warm in California. He wondered if, during my visit to Mr. Bennett's Sherborne, I had noticed how cold it was?

I assured him that it was fine: "It's pleasant there in June. Not so cold then."

He had visited Sherborne Center the previous year during the winter, and it had been very damp and cold. But he added that he knew of my good common sense and knew I would take care and make the right decisions.

I kept asking myself, if he was friends with Mr. Bennett, why did he keep telling me that England was so very cold? And what decisions was he talking about?

The next evening, the mother of the home where I was now staying cooked a traditional Turkish, multi-course meal. Unaware of the vast number of courses to come, from the hors d'oeuvres onward I took much larger portions than any Turkish person would dare. As the final courses were presented, I refused to take any more.

That night, stuffed, I slept in the room of Mr. Shushud's son. The wrapping paper taped to the wall kept catching my attention. Was his son interested in cars? Had he received a gift he wanted to remember? Was America special to him? The paper was so cheesy. Mr. Shushud meticulously covered each of his books with gold paper, so *he* couldn't have put it there. What kind of guy was this son, anyway?

The next morning at breakfast, I described the comedy of getting so full that I had to refuse food.

Mr. Shushud was clear: The woman couldn't give me her thoughts because she didn't speak English. She could only give me her food. I was to take it.

After a short pause, he resumed his explanation of Itlak. On the Itlak path, he said, you must be fully involved in life, including working, getting married, having children. Life is what burns you.

He fell silent, and tears slipped down his cheeks. "You must learn patience, my child."

He asked how I found my accommodations in his son's room. Had I noticed "the fine paper of wheels" next to my bed?

I told him I had but didn't share my judgment of it.

He returned to a discussion of fasting as an excellent means of spiritual progress. *What about fasting?* I thought. *Wasn't stuffing yourself exactly the opposite of what you're supposed to do?*

He emphasized the importance of remaining always skeptical, and he tied fasting with skepticism by explaining that with patience, fasting would bring new insights. Before direct experience, a person on "this road" should not believe what anyone else tells them.

At that point, he showed me zikr, a type of breath control. He did zikr continually during our conversations, whenever he wasn't speaking, and I soon learned that that accounted for many of his silences. He said we would talk more about zikr later.

I asked him if there were any Itlak groups and he said, no, it wasn't organized like that. None of this was anything like I had expected, and I was relieved to be going to Sherborne.

The following week, Mr. Shushud made arrangements for me to spend a few days with a family who had a summer home on the beach in Florya. The house was huge. They had a washer and dryer and a cook who tried to teach me how to make böreği, a type of puffed pastry affair. We ate all the time—delicious food. We didn't take advantage of the beach, but rather spent time with the family and other guests who came for tea and dinner and lunch every day. To be sure, there was never any fasting.

The mother didn't speak English, but according to one of the daughters who was about my age and who did, their mother was part of a group of women who met with Mr. Shushud at his home on a fairly regular basis. The daughter repeatedly told me how lucky I was to speak with Mr. Shushud privately and that he had shown me zikr. What did he and I talk about? I told her, although I don't remember exactly what I said; I believe I did mention that we often discussed my future plans.

She exclaimed on more than one occasion, "You didn't say *that* to him, did you?!" I was a bit mortified that I had apparently been so disrespectful. It didn't help matters any when the mother also indicated through her English-speaking daughter how important it was to be respectful of Mr. Shushud. I spent considerable time ruminating on how disrespectful I must have seemed to him.

When I was ready to leave, the mother gave me gold earrings and a pendant—all in the shape of the traditional hat worn by the whirling dervishes. Heavy and lovely they were, but I was uncomfortable with the gift. Surely, it was a misunderstanding. I had nothing to do with Mevlana or any dervish, for that matter.

In any case, when I got back to III Levent, I stood at the door scared to death and most subdued. Mr. Shushud looked puzzled. We moved into our regular places on the settee and parlor chair. After about five minutes of my silence, Mr. Shushud exclaimed, "My child, what is wrong with you? You are no fun anymore."

With that, the Florya family concerns were washed away. I asked him what he did to pass his days, and he said he studied. He mentioned that some people visited him and he wrote letters. Bennett was one of the people who visited him, and he, in turn, had visited Sherborne. He asked me if I knew various people from Sherborne, which of course I didn't since I hadn't started there yet. As usual, he was quite complimentary about Mr. Bennett and his experiences with him.

He again mentioned his friend from Detroit, Michigan, where "they make fine American cars."

I showed him the earrings and pendant and asked if he would talk about the dervishes.

He returned to the importance of fasting and doing zikr, then counseled me that I needed to go "droit, tout droit" for at least fifty years, that "this road" was long and hard. "But if you do not neglect zikr and fasting, they will not neglect you."

The next day, Mr. Shushud announced that he was taking me to see a few sites in Istanbul that he thought I might find interesting.

The first stop was a small museum where on display were the elaborately carved doors to the house of Mevlana Jalaluddin Rumi. Mr. Shushud spoke of Mevlana's greatness. Mevlana was buried in Konya, Turkey, and the Mevlana Museum in Konya was an important place to visit. One day I must visit it, he told me.

Our second stop was the Topkapi Palace. We only stopped in three of the rooms there. The first had displays of porcelain from China and the robes of famous Turkish sultans. The second had, in its own special case, the arm of John the Baptist ensconced in some type of precious metal. And the third was the Pavilion of the Sacred Mantle—the mantle of the Prophet Mohammed. We stayed the longest in these last two rooms.

Mr. Shushud clearly wanted me to see the arm of John the Baptist. He prayed over it, then commented that since I had been born a Christian, the arm was of particular significance. I looked at it long and hard without much result, and therefore with much disappointment.

In the third room, Mr. Shushud prayed at length in front of the mantle. His love and respect were obvious, but he didn't provide any conversation.

After lunch, we paid a visit to the Grand Bazaar. He took me to a couple of stalls where he knew the owners, and he helped me purchase a prayer rug. When we got back to his home, he talked about zikr.

He reminded me of his friend "in your great country," in Detroit, Michigan. His friend would visit soon, and this friend would show me how to do more zikr. I could do zikr on my prayer rug, although that was not necessary. The only thing that *was* necessary was to do zikr.

Now that he was talking about zikr, I asked him to describe more about Itlak. There wasn't much to explain. There were no ceremonies, no rules, no regulations, no best way to be. Only fasting, zikr, suffering, and discussion, and the last was the least important, since everything was based on individual experience.

As usual, I thought how lucky I was to be committed to Sherborne. When I reminded Mr. Shushud that I had to return to England soon, he responded as usual, "You must learn patience, my child."

During my final week, Mr. Shushud informed me that I would be joining the family across the street on their visit to their relatives in Bursa. We would only stay one night. The father of the family we were to visit was a taxi driver, so he would provide all the transportation. This would include a ferry ride, which gave us an excellent view of Istanbul with its minarets and the Bosporus.

When we arrived in Bursa, we went directly to the relatives' home. They had, if I remember correctly, five children, and one set of grandparents who also lived in the home. The house that they lived in consisted of three rooms: An all-purpose room for living, dining, and sleeping, a room the size of a closet that served as the kitchen, and a third room the size of a closet that served as the bathroom. Throughout, the floors were packed dirt, although there were rugs on the floor in the living room. There was no running water, and there was no real workspace in the tiny kitchen, so the grandmother sat on the living room floor, with a board on her lap, making dolmas. We had quite a feast, and I remember how important it was to keep eating. (What struck me years later was that thanks to Mr. Shushud, I was able to stay with a rich family, a poor family, and a middle-class family, and all of them were essentially the same.)

It took all morning to get back to Istanbul from Bursa. When I arrived back at Mr. Shushud's home, Nuriye Hanim opened the door as usual, but this time she was flurried with excitement. She motioned me into the front door and through to the living room. There, Mr. Shushud was standing with a stocky Turkish man with a moon-shaped face. "Come and meet the good doctor from Detroit," he said with an open arm. Then, turning to the doctor and gesturing to me, "This is Lilly."

The doctor responded, "I will send you an airplane ticket." After a pause, he added, "I'm sure we will get along famously."

He was just leaving, because he had a plane to catch back to Detroit. Apparently, they had been waiting for me.

So this is what all this has been about, I thought. *What on earth are they thinking? What am I supposed to tell Bennett? And why don't any of these people use more words?* I took my backpack up to "my" room, then descended to protest. This must be some sort of test to see if I was really committed to Bennett's school and to my spiritual progress. I was feeling, as my dear mother would say, fit to be tied.

"You must think of your mother. You will have to pay if you go to England. If you go to Detroit, the good doctor will pay you. You will teach at his school." Mr. Shushud had already shared with me that the doctor was starting a pre-school in Michigan.

"But all my friends are going to be in England, and I teach French and English in secondary school, not pre-school."

"Remember how cold it is in England."

"But my boyfriend will be there."

"Look carefully at your situation, my child. Visit the doctor in Detroit. He will send you a ticket. See what situation he will offer you. Consider well. You have traveled enough. It is time to settle down. Be at home. Find out what that means." After a pause he added, "Remember the wheels on the wallpaper in your room. They are a sign that you belong in the great city of Detroit." After another pause, he added, "But you will sleep on this."

Go figure. That night I had a dream that I was teaching four-year-olds and loving my new job. So, the next day after I'd "slept on it," my decision was made. I would go to Detroit, at least to check things out.

In our final conversations, Mr. Shushud told me to follow the good doctor's instructions as to exactly how to fast and how to do zikr.

He told me that the first three years would be the most difficult, but that if I went "droit, tout droit," and did as the good doctor instructed me, I would be on the Itlak road.

He counseled me that I should fast and do zikr and wait for them to provide me with firsthand experiences. "Above all, my child, you must remain always skeptical. Use your good sense and conscience to decide. Do not believe what anyone else tells you on this road, but wait until you experience it yourself."

He suggested I refer to *Conference of the Birds* and the *I-Ching*, a book I already relied on when I was feeling unsure of myself. These would make the time pass more quickly and softly and, most important, would be reminders that the spiritual road is a long one.

I finally made a plane reservation to go back to England, where I shared the news of the new plan with Mr. Bennett, who seemed neither surprised nor inconvenienced. I then flew to Detroit to meet with Dr. Nevit Ergin once more, in order "to see my situation," flew home to visit my family, then drove across country to Michigan to set up house-keeping with whatever belongings I could fit in my Volkswagen Beetle.

If you, the reader, are noting that my interactions with Mr. Hasan Shushud could be characterized as those of a foolish young girl meeting a kind, wise old man, you are correct. However, as should be evident from the body of this book, to consider him only as a kind, wise old man would be to underestimate him exponentially.

It took only three weeks for him to get me to change my mind completely as to what road I would be taking. Even believing that my decision was the correct one, for my first three years in Detroit, I fought the simplicity, the bare bones of Itlak, a path that I found disconcerting at best. But it has saved me from endless wrong turns and serious dead ends.

On the Itlak road, the only thing to do is to fast, do zikr, take your suffering slowly, and show up every day. What is it in our nature as humans that makes us crave ceremony, groups, explanations? Why do we think that a guide of any kind, that any other human being on this planet, has the answers, and that "they" can bring us enlightenment and that we shouldn't have to do the work for ourselves?

I recorded as best I could the key events and conversations that occurred while I was visiting with Mr. Shushud; however, much to my regret, I rarely recorded his exact words.

We didn't talk about Mevlana's work, although he referred to Mevlana constantly. Nor did we talk about anything from Mr. Shushud's own book, *Masters of Wisdom of Central Asia,* although he did talk about the fact that he had written the book and suggested I try to get a copy, "when it was the right time." I don't believe it had been translated into English in 1972. He also told me that it wasn't that I would get answers to all my questions, but that I would simply lose my questions.

I begged so much for "information," that he did write out a few sayings on index cards and gave them to me while I was in Turkey, but he didn't give them to me all at once, and I didn't keep them in any order. However, those sayings are noted verbatim here:

Existence is a reality, but reality is unreal.

The meaning of creation is a perception.

Marriage is a collision of two universes.

The Universe is a splendid lie. What is life? An agony.

If you know the world, you don't try to improve it.

If you are pleased with what you have found, that is good. If you are not, this is much better.

As he had advised me, the first three years on the Itlak road were the most difficult, and for those three years, he wrote me letters of encouragement. They included the following:

L'égo est un "produit" de nos organes et de leur fonctionnement. Personne ne peut y changer grand chose. Itlak se trouve sur un tout autre plan. Tout en restant dans le "frame" de religion léguee par nos parents et ancêtres et observant as a compass—la conscience et le bon-sens, nous constaterons dans notre coeur et âme des progrès surprenants avec le temps. Et chaque pas confirmera les précédents . . .

My translation: The "ego" is a product of our organs and their functioning. No one can change much. Itlak provides a completely different plan. All rests in the "frame" of the religion bequeathed by our parents and ancestors and observed as a compass—with conscience and good sense—we ascertain in our heart and soul astonishing progress with time. And each step will confirm the previous one.

So that for me was the beginning. What I have found in the past forty-some years is that this business isn't *anything* like I thought it would be. The Self is insidious, despicable, the worst kind of weed in the garden. It thrives on psychology, religion, science, philosophy, education, whatever culture you were born into, whatever in this world you are drawn to . . . whatever. No amount of wishful thinking, set of beliefs, pampering, pulling, or applying pesticides (organic or otherwise) can get rid of it; if left alone, it takes over everything. Fasting and zikr (and the suffering that follows) are the key to its slow but sure eradication.

I will be eternally and deeply, humbly grateful to Hasan Shushud and to Nevit Ergin, the wonder man Mr. Shushud introduced me to in Turkey, for giving me their friendship, the poetry of Mevlana, and the Itlak practices. Far more important, however, the work they have accomplished is beyond reckoning. They are inspirational proof that it is possible to make it, that this business isn't some joke but something to be taken deadly seriously.

PART 6

On Perception

Sayings

Poems

A Story: Skunk

An Essay: Creation and Perception

Questions and Answers about Perception

Sayings

✳

Hasan Lutfi Shushud

Perception is the most important abstract concept that manifests infinite layers of limited awareness of totality.

The description of dualistic perception: Infinite layers of limited awareness of the totality—absolute.[1]

The unannihilated person tastes non-dualistic perception in the dream sleep. "Being" becomes free from the bondages of time and space. Annihilation produces a dreamlike perception permanently.

We are all the children of our Perception.[2]
And, the Universe is the shadow of the Perception.[3]

The universe shares the characteristics of existence and non-existence. The ones who experience the world only by their senses see material, physical objects. But, the ones who are annihilated see the world of potentiality, occult objects (objects of knowledge).[4]

With non-dual perception, perceiver and perceived become the same as the opposite of the unannihilated human perception, where there are perceivers and perceived.

Totality is God's knowledge of himself as an undifferentiated whole. Above this lies the mysteries of the mysteries.[5]

When Perception is the first primordial and non-dual stage (no perceiver, no perceived), there is manifested an infinite number of universes by infinitely different awarenesses. Who made it like that? It is the mystery of mysteries. Unless one changes their perception from dualistic to non-dualistic perception, it will remain a mystery.

Non-dual perception has been known for a long time in Vedanta, Buddhism, and Taoism under the name of "Advaita." Some believe Vedic sacrifices and devotional worship can lead one whose perception will dissolve the Atman (self) into Brahman (essence of self, utter consciousness, infinite wholeness). In Itlak Sufism, this change in perception is obtained only by annihilation of the self.

Poems

Mevlana Jalaluddin Rumi

One who has boarded a sailing boat sees that trees
    are moving.
It is like that: We are passing by, through the world,
But we think that the world is passing us.[6]

I said, "My heart is so small that it isn't even seen
    among the visible.
How can Your big sorrow fit into it?"
He answered, "Look at your eye. That is also small,
But don't big things fit in there?"[7]

For the one who knows the true nature of Existence
    and Non-Existence,
Being and Non-Being can trouble him.
The one who is free from creation and turns into
    Creator
Isn't bothered by acts and attributes.[8]

A Story

Skunk

Nevit O. Ergin

My life has changed since that day—the day I found a dead skunk in my backyard.

As soon as I found it, I called the proper places for help. They told me either to bring the carcass over to them or to bury it myself.

Naturally, I buried it myself.

I put on double gloves, double masks. I dug a deep hole next to the body. I rolled it over into the hole and put plenty of soil on top. Then, I took a long shower. Unfortunately, all the soaps and body sprays I could get my hands on didn't take the smell away.

My wife and my son picked up the smell. I told them the story and added, "A live skunk stinks, but a dead skunk is offensive." My wife not only closed her bedroom door, but made sure my bedroom door was closed. My son hesitated when he gave me a good-night kiss.

Shortly after that day, fall came. My wife moved to a sunny place and my son found a new girlfriend, so he came home late, and always just to sleep.

Accepting old age, a time for compromise and abandonment, made me resigned, even gave me solace. I knew I had no chance in this particular set of realities. I had to retreat to a new world. Death is the only itinerary for humans. Could I die while I was still alive?

I thought about this very seriously, and I asked for help. Most of the people I asked didn't answer when I posed the question, but looked at me strangely. Some wondered, "How can you be dead and at the same time alive? Life and death don't go together."

Everyday life dazzled my eyes and senses, and reasoning tied my hands. I was encouraged not to explore beyond that. But stories of human successes and failures are all based on the transient values of life. I asked myself, if no one owns anything, why is there so much fighting? Even the air we take in, with every breath we give back. Life is a one-way, dead-end street. Everything we do ends up on this dead-end street. But people are busy day and night for buying, selling, and moonlight. Who fooled them into forgetting the inevitability of death?

How could I explain that the particles that make up my body have no time-space boundary? They swim in Nothingness. If I could change my perceptions from my body to my particles, I could experience immortality. The question was how to change my perception.

I remembered the body of the dead skunk. It didn't breathe and didn't eat. Maybe the secret was in there.

I woke up in the morning to the familiar sound of a cat. I opened the door. It was my old black cat, Karacan. I said, "Karacan, how did you come here? I thought you were killed by the skunk."

I went to get milk. On my return Karacan was not there. I looked everywhere. I called its name. It had disappeared into nowhere.

I realized then that the very same animal had appeared to me as a skunk one day and another day as a black cat. The victim and villain had become the same. Gradually, the difference between good and bad had narrowed down. The lover had become the Beloved; creature had become creator.

I went out for a short while. When I returned to the house, I found a man in my room. I was surprised and scared and asked,

"How did you get in here?" He pointed to the open terrace door. I always felt something like that would happen one day. Somehow, intentionally, I had neglected to close the door.

He was sitting at my desk, looking at my computer. My papers were scattered all around.

"Did you write all this?" he asked angrily.

"Yes," I said.

"Aren't you ashamed?" Then he added: "Do you know any prayers?"

I shook my head.

"You are a heretic, and I'm going to kill you."

His voice was calm, his eyes were knife-sharp. I felt a chill all over me. "Can we talk?" I asked.

"No. Besides, you stink. I'm going to blow apart every bone in your legs. You won't be able to move. I'm going to cut your wrists. You will die slowly by bleeding. I'm going to close your mouth with tape. You won't be able to call for help."

"Why not shoot here?" I pointed to my heart.

"That would be doing you a favor."

I couldn't help but ask, "Why do you hate me so much?"

He finally explained the reason for his actions. "You and I cannot be in the same house."

I said calmly, "This is my house."

"How do you know that?"

Then, I realized the conversation about anything beyond the house was dead.

He continued, "You are like a hair in my eye, a thorn in my foot. If I don't eliminate you, I won't see anything, won't go anywhere." He paused. I looked at his face. "You are my Self."

How could I blame this gentleman?

An Essay

Creation and Perception

Nevit O. Ergin

The soul is just a fish,
Wishes and desires are God's fishing line.
What a wonderful thing this desire is,
A fisherman that sacrifices souls.

The ant doesn't have wings, but wishes to fly
And pierce the wall of Love's palace.
Don't call him an ant because of ignorance.
He wants a throne, a crown.
He demands to be Sultan.

There was God
Before the Universe was even created.
Why did He desire to bring us here?
I don't know.

This desire is such that
We are neither part of it,
Nor is it different from us.

O Shams to whom Tabriz praises,
You untie this knot.[9]

If Absence were not subjugated
By the majesty of your order,
No existence could ever appear
In this land of despair.[10]

Creation has remained the greatest mystery for mankind. Neither the colorful stories in the sacred testaments nor the theories in science books have surpassed beyond poetry and mental abstraction (although present-day quantum mechanics is much closer to mysticism than Newtonian physics).

Didn't your grandfather Adam
Come to this world
Because of the wheat?
The heart and mind follows the tune of
    the self;
It naturally falls into separation.[11]

Maybe the reason for this impasse is that all of these assumptions have a common idea about the origin of the universe. "Something" was created from "nothing." This makes "nothing" like "something," putting the two in the same category.

One who realizes this dichotomy stays away from its realm. But most pursue and form all kinds of theories. Nothingness should not be subject to our perspective, our point of view. We should never extend linear causality to an infinite beginning and infinite end.

The Light is the creator of reason.
Every reason is in this shadow.
God made "no reason"
The reason for everything.[12]

Divinity, no matter how abstract it is, becomes a subject for humans' minds. The frustration and dissatisfaction usually follows the answers of major questions (for example: life and death, creator and creatures). This is a natural result of our inability to comprehend. "The Universe has not passed beyond potentiality."[13]

> The one who is heedless is in the deep coma
>   of Creation.
> The meaning of Creation is Perception,
> And the world is the shadow of Perception.[14]

Accepting the Creation as a fact splits the wholeness, the Unity, into a creator and creature, Lover and Beloved. Although this explains our longing for completion, it also creates the problem of how to go with this yearning for union. The created universe in our particular human perception is the potentiality that transcends "everything else"—God.

> Whoever says we are One,
> We will put him in the gallows.
> But whoever says we are two,
> We will throw him into the fire.[15]

> You are the One who says, "you are."
> You are the ball on the field,
> You are the club.
> You are the One who watches the game.[16]

> He is the One who desires everyone,
> Yet He is called, "The One who is desired."
> He worships everyone,
> Yet He is called, "The One who is
>   worshipped."[17]

Your soul is the *Muezzin* [preacher] and *Kayyum*
    [caretaker] of your body's mosque.
Prostration is concealed in the attribute of "being
    prostrated."[18]

In occult visions, Perception is infinitely rich, not only in humans, but also before and after humans. Variations of perception in different forms of existence is called Presence (*Hazerat*). One experiences the Universe differently depending on the stage of this Perception.

Instead of wasting time indulging in endless discussions of "Evolution vs. Creation," which ends up in a dead end anyway, one should try to change his Perception. How? By "being his own martyr."[19] Then one can experience the divine secrets that have been hidden from him.

Absence and Existence fluctuate with a rhythm so fast that no one could ever perceive it with three dimensions and a time- and space-bound mind. This ignorance is the source of our earthly comfort and wisdom.

We only see the dust, but never the wind.[20]

In the land of separation,
The one who cannot see Your face
Accepts "reason" and a *Kible* [direction].
For the blind, it is better to have a cane
Than a candle.[21]

But, there is another layer of Perception:

A door was opened to me from Absence
Before I had ever been created,
Before I came from Nothingness
To the circle of beings.[22]

One moment you put us to sleep.
The next, you send us to reason.
One moment you throw us to the world of
    existence,
The next to the desert of Absence.[23]

I am the *Ye'juj*, I am the *Me'juj*.*
I am the Absolute One with infinite numbers.[24]

                              •

---

*Old Testament 38-39-Coc-Macoc: Old Testament X-20 Comer-Me'juj. Koran XVIII
94–100 Zulkarneyn

Questions and Answers about Perception

Q: What do you mean by "human perception"?
A: There are unlimited layers of perception before humans and after humans. Our human perception is a dualistic perception. God is the unmanifested part of it. The cosmos is the manifested part.

Q: Can you give an example of how our human perception works?
A: Human perception creates time and space, senses, mind, body, causality, and many other things. The mind creates certain rules, and out of those rules, causality comes first.

Q: What is the origin of our human perception?
A: We inherited this perception through evolution, and it doesn't culminate with human beings. There are unlimited layers of perception before and after human beings. Each one of those layers has a limited awareness of the Truth.

Q: Is the Self what keeps us bound in our human perception?
A: Self is the product of human perception, and Self is the curse of humanity.

Q: And you're saying we can change our human perception by doing certain practices that directly impact our body?

A: Our body is the only thing we have. The difference between a dead body and a live one is eating and breathing. Manipulating those two functions has a profound effect on perception. We're not talking about starvation or suffocation. But working on one's body makes it possible to die before one's chronological death. Otherwise, as Mevlana says, we're just "a morsel for the ground."

Q: How do you know when you've reached a new level of perception?
A: It's all a process. Changes in perception happen bit by bit over time, gradually, just like the seasons change, grass grows, and day turns into night. It doesn't happen in one split second or with a drumbeat. Eventually, one has full control of time and space. One can be in two places at the same time. Past, present, and future are combined.

Q: Since we share human perception, is it possible for humans to perceive things in the same way?
A: No. We are the children of our perception. Each child is different. Although we share human perception, none of us see things the same way. This is the reason for our universal misunderstandings.

Q: Is there anything that is not a product of our perception?
A: Nothing at all. Everything is a result of our perception. This is all perception. Perception is everything.

PART 7

On Death

Sayings

Poems

A Story: Assassins

Questions and Answers about Death

Sayings

Hasan Lutfi Shushud

Death is the poem of the universe.[1]

Human beings are asleep; they only wake up at death.[2]

Jump into the bottomless abyss that you be free from the fall, like stars in the sky.[3]

The thing you lost at your birth, you will find at your death.[4]

Waves appear, disappear in the sea, are neither born nor die. Death and birth are the same.[5]

Genuine Sufism is the quest for truth by mystical revelations and transformational experience. There is no way to achieve this but by voluntary death, that is: "Die before you die."[6]

All we know about death are accounts of the surviving ones. The ones who die carry away the mystery forever. We should be serious about this question, because death is the only truth in our lives. Who makes us forget this fact? Everyone thinks about someone else's death, not their own.

Poems

Mevlana Jalaluddin Rumi

The dilapidated house of your life has been
    flooded.
The glass of your time is getting full.
Relax. In the twinkling of your eyes,
The warden of time will move your belongings
    from the old house.[7]

Hear this advice: Try hard for two or three days
    to die,
Two or three days before your death.
This world is an old woman left over from many
    husbands.
Wouldn't it be better not to waste your two or
    three days with that old woman?[8]

You became so intimate with your soul,
Who is a guest of your body for a couple of days.
You don't want to listen to my talk about death.
But your soul is yearning for its halting place—
    the death before death.

Unfortunately, your body's donkey fell asleep in
the middle of the road.[9]

There is a new life in death for the man of
justice and faith.
Peace and calm come from death to clean souls.
Death is reaching to God, not fear and tortures.
The one who won't die with this kind of death
will die every day.[10]

There are thousands of deaths buried in that
house.
You sit on the top of them, saying, "There are all
my belongings."
A handful of dust says, "I used to be hair."
Another says, "I used to be bone."
You become confused. Suddenly, Love comes and
says:
"Come close to me, I am immortal. Put your
chest over my silver chest,
Embrace me. I will save you from yourself."[11]

Soul flies out of the body at the time of Death,
Throws away the body like an old dress.
The body made by dust goes back to dust.
Soul makes a new body with his old radiance
And dresses him with new flesh.[12]

A Story

Assassins

Nevit O. Ergin

Most of the time I had been aware that someone was following me. I had heard the approaching footsteps of the invisible person. Gradually my fear turned into annoyance; I couldn't get away from my pursuer. The more I tried to rush, the more I slowed down. Neither vitamins nor special diets energized me. Then I accepted that the footsteps have been a part of my life rather than a threat. They are like echoes of my footsteps.

I have witnessed the death of friends and family members. After the initial shock and mourning, a deafening silence comes from somewhere and covers everything like snow. All of the rituals and mythologies about death are for the survivors. What happens to the one who dies is the great mystery, buried in Nothingness. Yet this issue occasionally confronts us in everyday life. They are not matters for the mind, but reason still fabricates comforting explanations by extending causality before birth and after death.

At the end of the day, I had run out of everything worth thinking about and doing. So sleep came to my mind as a last blessing. I quickly took off the clothes that the day had put on me and slipped into bed.

I stayed awake for so many hours so I could have this sleep. The only freedom man has is to dream, where time and space are two useless accessories of life. I felt light and free, like a feather on an evening breeze. I started dreaming in a starless, pitch-black evening. I was standing on the edge of a cliff.

Then the doorbell rang a few times. I pretended I didn't hear it and tried to incorporate it into my dream. But the doorbell rang again and I got up. I was mad, but at the same time curious.

When I opened the door, I saw a man dressed in black. He handed me a small package and said, "Special delivery."

"I didn't know there were still deliveries at this time," I said.

The answer came calmly, "Twenty-four hours."

I waited for him to leave, but instead he asked if he could come inside. "You may need some help in your dream."

I remembered the dream: I was standing at the top of the cliff in the darkness of a starless night. I sensed there was a sea deep below. I was hesitating between the temptation of self-annihilation and the addicting pleasures of temporal things in daily life.

"How did you know about my dream?" I asked.

"That's where I live," he said. "I work when everyone is awake."

"But," I asked, "who are you?"

"A special delivery man," he said calmly. "I deliver people's belongings and take their soul."

"Can I call you an 'unholy assassin' then?" I asked.

He wasn't offended.

I took him inside. "My son is sleeping, we shouldn't wake him," I said.

When we got to my room, I had all kinds of questions. Is there something more than death? If I was going to die, why was I born? How true is the story of heaven and hell? I had many more, but what was the use of asking them? I was about to find out for myself.

I tried to be conciliatory. Remembering the old movie, *The Seventh Seal,* I asked, "Do you play chess?"

"I'm not so good," he answered.

"How about backgammon?"

He hadn't heard of it. "Come on now," he said, "one little push won't hurt. Death is a road that you have never travelled."

"Yes, I have. But only halfway."

He looked at my face.

"I'm writing a book called *How To Die Before Death*," I told him.

"Do you want my job?" he asked angrily.

"How can I? You are appointed for all mortals. They want to be immortal, but gradually die by changing their eating, breathing and using the fire of suffering."

"But," he said, "I see a lot of you are still here."

"Changing perception takes a long time. I started this book forty years ago. Maybe no one will read it; I just want to finish it." I realized this wasn't his concern.

I turned off the light and went to bed, knowing he was still in the room. I was scared, tired, and frustrated. It didn't take long before I fell asleep, and my dream was the same as before. I was standing on the edge of a cliff. I knew I could not return. A saying came to my mind, "The one who loves to fall in Nothingness finds that God is the Abyss."

I threw myself into the darkness.

When I opened my eyes, I was in the emergency room. The rest of the story came from my son.

He woke to a scream that was coming from my room. He found me on the floor in agony, as I showed him my big toe. All I could say was, "Something bit me there." Using a flashlight to examine the bed, he found the guilty one: the assassin, a bedbug. The black spot rushed to find a place to hide. Using the back of my slipper, my son smashed it on the white sheet, along with my dream of immortality.

I opened that little box that came as a "special delivery." Inside was a handful of ashes and dirt, as if to say, "Before you become like this, hurry up and finish the book."

Questions and Answers about Death

Q: Can you provide a bit more insight into the nature of death?
A: We should be serious about this question, because death is the only truth in our lives. Who makes us forget this fact? Why does everyone think about someone else's death, but not their own? Why are humans afraid of death? Death is the Absolute Reality, the Absolute Truth.

All we know about death are accounts of the ones who survive. The ones who die carry away the mystery forever.

Q: How would you define "to die before you die"?
A: This means to go beyond our Self, beyond human perception, and then come back and still have human perception. A fish doesn't know water unless he goes up in the air, lives there for a while, and then returns to the water. At that moment he knows air *and* water.

Now if a person dies before their chronological death, they'll know about death and life.

Q: So you believe "dying before your death" is our best option?
A: If we don't manage to die before we die, in other words, to change our perception from our body to our Essence, we'll be dying with the fear of death every single day. That fear follows us like an assassin. It doesn't matter if we're living in a church or a mosque or a temple or anywhere else. This journey to die before we die is beyond faith, beyond

heresy. Religious paradise is simply an imagined extension of our earthly pleasures.

Q: Does our soul live after our physical body dies?

A: At the human level of perception, we create time and space. Naturally, when we're born into time and space, we also have to die. We have a physical body. That's the result of our perception. We're addicted to our physical body, so naturally, we don't want to give it up. The body is our worshiping element. We do everything to please the body, and it's very difficult for us to understand the idea of death without pain.

We don't know the experience of the one who dies. All our notions of the experience of death are simply part of the game our human perception plays with us. Absolutely nothing like what we imagine about death actually happens. There is no way to understand this problem with the mind. We do not know death until we die first. That's what this book is all about.

Death and birth happen every split second, but we're not aware of it. We see only a continuous life. This is exactly the fallacy our human perception has created. In Annihilation of Actions, one doesn't see body, one sees spirit, one sees soul. This is why we say it is necessary to change our perception from bodily to "particle" perception. Actually, we do have this particle perception, but we don't see it. We're floating in Nothingness. We just don't see it. We see only a time- and space-bound body perception, and, unfortunately, we're used to that.

Q: Does the path prepare for a life after death?

A: What is life after death? The common understanding of death only remains for the ones who survive. None of the descriptions or explanations of death comes from the one who dies. We don't hear their statement, their tale, their story. Survivors might imagine their own body being eaten by ants, worms, all kinds of bad things. And we think we're in the process of settling down in a better location than the one who has just died. We look to religion, do whatever we think is necessary.

Q: What about reincarnation?

A: Reincarnation is an earthly term we use after we accept existence. As such, it explains many things to us. But if we don't accept Existence, what is the use of reincarnation?

Q: Do you have any final words?

A: Some of us are not satisfied with the human rationalization of what happens before birth and after death and the theory of causality, so we search for our Essence by changing our perception. We try to go beyond the structure of time and space. We see that our body is made of particles. Sometimes these particles are here and sometimes they're there. They certainly have no space and time boundary. And if we go even deeper, we get to Nothingness. Our body is only one of an infinite number of perceptions. We don't have to live with our human perception. In any case, it's only temporary. Death always comes and closes it up.

PART 8

On Life

Sayings

Poems

A Story: Intersection

Questions and Answers about Life

Sayings

Hasan Lutfi Shushud

The external world is constructed by our sensory perception and intellectual comprehension.[1]

If you are happy with what you find, it is fine; if you are not, it is better.[2]

Things were born from nothing. They are still nothing, but they manifest like something in this world.[3]

Life is a magnificent lie; the universe is a magnificent waste.[4]

I hope you say, "I won't go the way I came from."[5]

Belonging to a nationality and society is a chance in vain.[6]

Your shadow is here, your Essence is at non-being.[7]

Matter and its Essence are the same.[8]

The life that is passing with pleasure is a waste. The life with sorrow is a treasure.[9]

Poems

Mevlana Jalaluddin Rumi

Cause and effect" are hot air to me.
How can you build a mud house on the sea?[10]

You are nothing, and "nothing" cannot be
    displayed to your eyes
As a something better than this.[11]

You showed Nothingness as an existence.
You hid the wind, showed the dust.[12]

Night has come; it is time for the people to fall
    asleep
Like the fish that plunges back into water.
In the morning, most will follow the steps of
    reason.
Only a few will walk toward the One who
    created reason.[13]

A Story

Intersection

Nevit O. Ergin

I have been at this intersection for a long time. I don't know how many times the light has changed. Every time the light turns green for me, I start to cross the street but get stopped violently by the people coming in the opposite direction. There are so many of them, walking faster than me and more anxious to make it to the other side. My age and physical condition haven't impressed anyone. They just drag me back to the sidewalk where I stood before.

I was feeling like I was in an ant colony. They were the ants with a specific mission, carrying out their tasks energetically. I was an old ant with no mission. Then I noticed this rather young crowd dressed differently; most of them held a cigarette in their left hand and a cell phone in their right. They were either talking or smoking in between conversations.

I thought of an alternate route to go home, then I realized I had no home. The home I lived in had been foreclosed on, and I had recently been evicted from the place I was renting. I was homeless, but alive. I wanted to tell everyone, "This will happen to each one of you. How come you don't believe in death? Who made you forget that? None of your dear ones will keep you in your home for more than a day when you die." I knew nobody would listen to me.

I felt better that I didn't have to cross the street. I turned and followed the crowd. It was easier to go with the flow. Someone pushed me to the side; I was about to step on a black cat lying on the crowded sidewalk. The person who pushed me said, "Can't you see?" The cat was pregnant, helplessly showing its fat belly as if asking for help.

It didn't resist when I picked it up and put it in my backpack. Though unexpected, my cargo gave me a sense of urgency and purpose. It seemed the kittens were ready to come.

My road ended in a busy parking lot. Several buses were loading people and luggage in a hurry. I approached the last bus, which was almost full. The driver was anxious to close the doors. Then I learned there was a golf tournament; the buses were carrying equipment and caddies. Someone yelled at me, "Don't stand there!" He then asked, while pointing at my backpack, "What's in it?"

"Cat," I said.

He corrected me, "Caddy. Get in." So I got in and sat in the back. I put my bag in front of me, hoping the delivery would be a quiet one. The bus took off and we gradually left the city. The scenery changed; flowers adorned the quiet country green. It was an amazingly welcome contrast to the city's hustle and bustle.

It was late in the afternoon when the bus stopped at the top of the hill, in front of a small building. The passengers all made their way to the clubhouse.

The course was situated in a valley, with a dominant green lawn and skillfully placed trees and water as accessories. I found a place to spend the night, and anxiously wanted to pull the cat from my backpack; it was quietly asleep in the pack. But when I put the backpack on the ground, the cat got out and walked toward the bushes, disappearing.

I lay down on the ground and slept by listening to the silent song of the stars. When I woke up in the early morning, there was a small spider in the air in front of me. It was putting on the most acrobatic show I had ever seen. I was still lying on my back, so I couldn't see the web it was hanging upside down from.

"Bravo, bravo," I said. "Where is your web?"

The spider smiled and waved to me. Like a trapeze artist swinging on a swing, it did a few other tricks before it sat on its web between two branches. I saw a big black bird at the top of that tree. It looked at me and asked, "Are you new here?"

"Yes," I said, "I am."

It took off yelling and screaming, "He's new! He's new!"

A crowd of sparrows came, along with a few squirrels, and looked at me. I didn't know whether I should get up and greet them. I waved, smiled, and bent my head. A white butterfly appeared and turned around me several times. I heard a sweet but simple birdsong coming from a small tree in front of me. I looked carefully but couldn't see the bird.

The butterfly above me asked, "Do you want me to show you where the bird is?"

It flew to the side of the tree, pointing to a small dark spot among the leaves. I thanked the butterfly.

A few ants then began to climb over me. A big one asked, "Are you an explorer?"

"Yes," I replied. What was wrong with being an explorer anyway?

I got up and tried to find the black cat. I found the corner where it had disappeared the previous night. It was still there in the bushes, and it recognized me. It was lying on its side, nursing five kittens. Its face had changed from being one of a tired, scared cat to that of a tired but happy mother cat.

I congratulated her and asked, "Why didn't you wake me up for help?"

"I didn't need it," she replied.

I remembered then that *Homo erectus* was disadvantaged when it came to childbirth; due to the effects of gravity the human uterus had to develop a strong cervix, and a human baby does not come easily. Nevertheless, motherhood fit all creatures and made them equal.

I spent the rest of the day around the golf course while the tournament was going on. I tried to express my appreciation for giving me the chance to live in such an environment rather than the city. Some people asked me, "Aren't you returning to town?"

"Sir," I replied, "I have no business and no place there. This is my home."

I slept in the same spot I had the night before. I again listened to the silent song of the stars and smelled the lilac trees.

Around midnight I woke up to the sound of the black cat screaming and lots of commotion. I ran in her direction with a flashlight and saw the masked face of a raccoon. It was standing and looked right at me. The black cat was bleeding from its face, trying to cover the kittens under her belly. After I tried scaring the raccoon, it eventually left. The cat welcomed my help; it was scared and breathing heavily. I stopped the bleeding on her face.

As I looked around with my flashlight, I saw it. A lifeless kitten. The cat was aware of this. "This is a crime," I cried. I turned to where the raccoon ran and yelled, "Murderer! Murderer!"

I couldn't sleep until dawn. I made a poster in the morning and took the cat with me. Every few steps I shook the poster and yelled, "The raccoon is a murderer!"

The people we met thought I was crazy. The birds did not understand what I was doing either. A stray dog asked me who the raccoon was, and I tried to explain, emphasizing the mask. He didn't know him, but asked, "What was the murder about?" I had a hard time making the dog understand the death. It had no idea about "life." It just shook its head and left me. After a while, the black cat also disappeared.

I felt like I was at an intersection in town.

Questions and Answers about Life

Q: You've spoken about death. What about its opposite . . . life?
A: What we call life is nothing but our imagination. When one wakes up, one sees it. We live half of our life in our sleep, as do all creatures. We dream when we wake up. When we sleep, we have no body, no time, no space. This is real life. Mr. Shushud always used to say, "Life is a magnificent lie." Annihilation is the key to seeing the validity of what he said. But, most people don't use that key, so they continue to think that the world exists. Once a non-dualistic perception is reached, life is seen as a magnificent lie and the universe as a magnificent waste. We're the ones making the world up. Some of us do see that.

Q: If you follow the path of Itlak can you still lead a normal life?
A: Mevlana talks about all roads in this world being dead-end streets. A one-way life is a dead-end street. The only way to get out of this dead end is this way: Dying before death. Annihilating one's Self.

Q: Does that mean one who is following the path won't have a normal life?
A: There is a saying, "The small monk goes up to the mountain; the big monk stays in the city." We firmly believe that an aspirant should hold a job, get married, have whatever is considered to be part of a normal life. But while we're in life, in family, in community, we keep one foot there

and the other foot in this area. Life and beyond life should go together. There is a popular saying: "While our hand is in the world, our heart is with the Beloved."

Q: Does that include the rules of morality?
A: All morality is a result of our perception. Itlak doesn't try to teach anyone anything about what is moral and what isn't. Suppressed, unwanted desires transform into different forms. No real change happens unless there is a change in perception.

PART 9

On Suffering

Sayings

Poems

A Story: No Shave, No Shower

Questions and Answers about Suffering

Sayings

Hasan Lutfi Shushud

We came as a guest to this house. We never met the owner. We have no idea where we were before or what we came for. Among the pains and pleasures, "self" was born here. With its mighty appetite, self has claimed everything as its own.

We forget that we are guests. The owner reminds us time by time by taking away the things that we are more attached to.

Suffering comes in the proper time to the aspirant. Knowing the reason for the suffering makes it more tolerable.

The cobblestones of this path have been paved by fire.[1]

Suffering is the most effective tool on this journey. Through suffering one understands that, "We are the bee; we are the honey."[2]

Likewise, we are the Lover; we are the Beloved.

Annihilation is the fruit of rigorous self-discipline and contrition [suffering].[3]

Occult visions:* Among the blessings of annihilation and the marvels of realization. Attained only through strict contrition [suffering] and spiritual exercises practiced over a long period of time.[4]

Contrition [suffering]: At the appropriate time and according to his ability to bear it, the Supreme Truth places the aspirant under a spiritual obligation to undergo detachment from the worlds of illusion and conditioning. This brings him to his pre-destined goal, the domain of reality and absolute liberation.[5]

The searing fire of contrition is the most effective instrument of spiritual progress. In the realm of the spirit, as in the material world, fire is a unique force of transformation and renewal. It must be faced by all who seek salvation.[6]

Contrition is a consuming fire for the carnal self, but it is life for the spiritual entity.[7]

---

*This definition of "occult visions" (Müşâhedât'i gaybiyye) is taken from the glossary section of Mr. Shushud's *Masters of Wisdom of Central Asia.*

Poems

Mevlana Jalaluddin Rumi

O one who wants the world, you are a
    day laborer.
O one who dreams of heaven, you are far
    away from the Truth.
O one who enjoys both worlds, but because
    of ignorance,
You haven't tasted the pleasure of His
    sorrow, you are excused.[8]

A moth, plunging into the fire,
Told me "Do the same."
He was burning, fluttering his wings
And telling me,
"Be like me."

The oil lamp is filled with oil.
Its wick is knotted, burning
With its broken neck,
And at the same time, telling me softly,
"Be like me."

The candle was burning and melting.
It gave itself for heat and suffering.
At the same time, it was telling me,
"Burn and melt like this.
Be like me."

"It isn't worth it to spend
Gold and silver to earn profit
In this world," he was saying.
"Try to burn. Melt this way.
Be like me."

The sea filled his lap with pearls,
Sat at the head, so as not to be conceited,
Showed itself bitter and salty.
It is trying to tell you,
"Be like me."

The Phoenix has given up good and bad,
Is free from traps.
It has settled down on Kafdagi,
Is trying to tell you,
"Be like me."

The rose purified its face,
Tore its robe, enduring the thorns,
Telling you to do and
"Be like me."

Wine gave up hundreds of names
And fame, free from shame and modesty,
Became an enemy to the mind,
Keeps running in man's brain,

Saying to you,
"Be like me."

The shrill pipe became completely empty,
Closed its eyes, only gave its lips
To the one who blows, and was saying
"Be like me."

Adam was in mourning forty years,
Kept crying, telling his children
"Be like me."

Be silent. Learn at last
A lesson from the hard rock.
It also stays silent, but cries
"Be like me."

See Shamseddin of Tebriz
Fill the valley with the light of Soul,
The plains with greatness, saying
"Be like me."[9]

A Story

No Shave, No Shower

Nevit O. Ergin

The spring was a touch of yellowish green, a promise on the trees. The ground was bare, sleepy, dotted with a few empty ant holes. I couldn't see the rising tide of spring in the branches yet. Neither could I hear the heartbeats of the plants and flowers still underground.

I did see the ships sailing on the invisible sea, carrying loads of illusions from nowhere to everywhere. Once they were crafted by the senses, the spring and seasons would appear in all their glory.

Since I have found myself on this side of the sea, time and place have become a constant headache. The caravan of causality never goes far in this land. It goes slowly at first, but later it breaks into many strange worlds. Reason is a key that opens many doors, but eventually, it becomes a lock.

Time is the worst villain among all man's adversaries. It gives the impression that it will last forever. It has no mercy at the end; it bends everyone's back. In time, gravity gets stronger, limiting movement so that finally a man's own weight becomes an unbearable burden. Either dimension or illusion, the time part of perception, is like a pair of tight shoes that one wears for so long. Sleep is the only relief—for all creatures. About half of life is spent without time and place; that's what's required to tolerate it.

I felt something crawling on my bare leg. It was a small ant. I watched for a while. When it noticed me watching, it changed direction. I picked it up. It stayed calm between my fingers; the reflex reaction of an ant is much kinder than that of other insects.

Nevertheless, after a short period of observation, I wanted to throw it away. One ant by itself doesn't have a likeable quality, but a colony represents a mighty, complex organism. I perceive the ants of a colony as a completely alien, extra-terrestrial existence.

The ant was not aware of any of that. Its life consisted of responding to chemical temptations. I looked around to see exactly where the holes in the ground were. I spotted a few, but no ants were around. I was sure the ant had lost its way and was asking me for help.

I was on the terrace. I thought that if I could get the ant onto the ground, it would find its way. I carried the ant three steps down into the garden. My age made it a long, hard walk, but I managed anyway.

After I left the ant on the ground, I decided to water the rose bushes. I slowly made it to the water spigot, turned on the water, but as I moved toward the rose bushes, I tripped on the hose as it lay in my path. I fell down.

Everything happened so fast. But, I do remember as I lost my balance, the fast-approaching ground. I landed face down. It felt like my bones were all right. I tried to get up. I couldn't. I tried again, to no avail. Crying for help didn't bring any results.

Since I was apparently stuck there, I turned my attention to the immediate neighborhood. I saw so many insects. Among them, there was my ant. He said, "You can't get through the hole, you're too big."

"What can I do?" I asked.

"Melt yourself like sugar."

The water, which I had intended for the rose bushes, was all around me. I saw sunflowers.

I let myself die.

What a relief. No shave, no shower tomorrow.

Questions and Answers about Suffering

Q: Exactly how does suffering come in?

A: An aspirant starts with fasting and then later adds zikr. The aspirant then reaches a certain stage where they're ready to take off. Suffering helps them to take off. Their balloon is already attached to the world with cords. Suffering cuts these cords one by one; it hurts them. When one's attachments to the world are cut, it goes with a lot of pain, not physical pain, but mental, psychological pain. In other words, whatever a person is attached to in this world—whether it's wealth, family, health, reputation—the hurt (from severing the attachment) will be a result of that attachment. If a person is famous, they'll be humiliated. If they have lots of wealth, they'll experience loss of wealth. If they have good health, they'll lose it. Wherever a person is weak, wherever their attachments are strongest, that's where they're going to get hit.

But again, if a person knows why this is happening, they can suffer through with pleasure. When they're ready, suffering cuts all of their ties, their attachments to the world, to reality. This puts a little wing on their shoulder.

Q: Would you say that suffering is more important than fasting or zikr?

A: Yes. Usually people who do a certain level of annihilation find out that breathing represents death and life, and that the particular period of zikr represents down-deep death, Nothingness, non-existence. If one uses that non-existence properly, they will change from bodily perception to particle perception. That's where annihilation is. That's what non-existence is; that's what our Essence is; that's what immortality is. If someone knows how to use that, they're saved from this temporary world. They die before their earthly death.

This is very important. It's as cheap and as simple as this. But ninety-nine percent of people breathe in and out and miss this part. Fasting and a different method of breathing (zikr) are the main tools of annihilation because they bring suffering.

Suffering is more important than fasting and zikr. Suffering is the fire that burns the Self. It is impossible to emphasize strongly enough the importance of suffering. One day of that suffering is equal to many years of fasting and zikr. To go through years of that suffering is equal to millions of years of fasting and zikr.

Q: How soon does suffering start?
A: Don't worry, when someone is ready, it will come. We start with fasting and zikr. They bring suffering.

Q: How do you tolerate suffering?
A: Praying makes suffering tolerable. It doesn't change suffering, but it makes suffering easier to tolerate.

Q: It sounds challenging. Is it difficult to stay on the path?
A: At the beginning, fasting and zikr become tiresome, and the aspirant needs to be reminded to persevere in doing the practices for about three or four or six months, depending on the person. After that, it's just like the flight of an airplane: After the plane reaches a certain altitude, it goes into autopilot. Likewise, after an aspirant does fasting and zikr for a certain period of time, the two practices take hold. The aspirant will continue to do them without being reminded. At that point, God will do the pulling.

PART 10

On Being and Becoming

Sayings

Poems

*A Story: Everything I Learned,
I Learned from a Mermaid*

*Questions and Answers about
Being and Becoming*

Sayings

Hasan Lutfi Shushud

Human perception is impressed by the system of Being and Becoming. This appears to the ordinary person as the universe. For the one who is annihilated, the universe is only potentiality, the capability of the Essence to know itself.[1]

Itlak is not learning, but unlearning.[2]

Contrary to earthly sciences, the answer doesn't come, but the question disappears.

Explanation changes the Truth.[3]

Truth must be experienced. You cannot talk about it; you cannot write a book about it; you cannot lecture about it. Language changes the truth.

Searching for the origin of something leads to the absence of everything.[4]

Nothing that has existed in the universe has gone beyond the possibility.[5]

Nothing that has existed in the universe can be destroyed because it has never been created.[6]

Creation has never happened.[7]

One who refuses to be born never dies.

The main thing is changing from existence to ecstasy.[8]

Annihilation of Essence is the completion of individualization. The journey by the way of Annihilation reaches God and goes beyond God. In the end of *Fenâ* [Annihilation], the beginning of *Baka* [Permanency] occurs. *Ke-en Lem Yekün* ["As if it were not"] is conferred.[9]

In summing up, Annihilation starts when existence ends. Annihilation ends at the secret of the Essence[10] and attainment of Non-being.[11]

Since man's behavior is the shadow of his Essence, all attempts to change the direction of the shadow are illusory. Nevertheless, mankind spends time and resources to do just that. Breadlessness, breathlessness are the cheapest things in the world. They are the best guide and make the one practicing them be exempted from the guide.[12]

A human's familial life, being, becoming, others, time and space, birth and death, creator–creatures, and the universe are all the products of this level of perception.

Upward progress from sense perception brings the realm of the spiritual world. Objects, corpuscular (bodily) appearances become a sense of possibility, then "objects of knowledge." Progress into this is the longest and hardest period. It ends with the Annihilation of Actions (*fenâ' al-af'âl*). This is the first degree of conscious death. It may last ten to twelve years depending on the aspirant and their adherence to the practices. Patience and persistence are necessary.

The second stage of annihilation is Annihilation of Attributes (*fenâ' al-ṣifât*). It is midway between Being and Non-Being. It is characterized by feelings of love and exuberance. Mevlana's love and ecstasy are a very good example of this.

Annihilation (*Riyazat*) is the actual process of changing perception. It is a slow, gradual affair by changing eating (fasting) and breathing (zikr) habits over time.

> The gradual destruction of the properties of being associates the gradual disappearances of the impression of the world and sense existence (here and now). They are replaced first by potentiality, then by non-existence through the stages of annihilation.[13]

> At the beginning, opposites are harmonized; blend in the perception by way of the alchemy of annihilation. This is symbolized by dawn and sunset. These stages of annihilation are experienced in actual reality, not mentally by reading or by listening.[14]

> Normal human perception has passed through the evolution of infinite previous layers and continues with infinite layers after that. Spiritual progress is accomplished through the process of being. Presences are the layers of being and are measures of the proximity to Essence.

> > Realm of matter (inorganic and organic materials, planets, and animals)
> > Sense perception (human)
> > Knowledge [*fenâ' al-af'âl*: first stage of Annihilation]
> > Relative mystery [*fenâ' al-ṣifât*]
> > Absolute mystery [*fenâ' al-dhât*]

These presences are accessible only by direct experiences. They are reached by gradual progress in self-annihilation.[15]

Poems

Mevlana Jalaluddin Rumi

Learned men said different things about Absence.
They pierced the pearls of wisdom on the way of
　　ignorance.
But, they were unable to understand the secret of
　　the Universe.
First, they wise-cracked, then they fell on the
　　ground and slept.[16]

The scholar who searches for truth behind this
　　door
Is like a piece of straw for Lovers.
The one who becomes master of his heart is in
　　the company of the Sultan.
The rest are pieces of straws.[17]

Since you don't become a Lover, go: Weave wool,
　　spin thread.
You change hundreds of colors and jobs.
Since there is no live wine in your skull,
Go, lick the bowls in the kitchen of the wealthy.[18]

Your Love makes knowledge a blunder.
What is Love? What is knowledge?
How can we know anyone?
While there is One we should find and know,
Both worlds are yelling, crying for Him,
Yet, we know nothing about Him.[19]

There is a different air in the gathering of Lovers.
There is a different drunkenness from Love's wine.
The knowledge you learned from school is one
      thing,
But Love is another matter.[20]

Better to be a fool of Love than a wise scholar.
If you are the moon in the sky, become dirt on
      this road.
Be together with good and bad, walk on the same
      road.
Be a pawn, the vizier, then a king later on.[21]

I was happy and cheerful with Your love.
When You left, my joy and happiness also left.
I was in such a mood with Your love that I
      couldn't recall Your love!
"Cause and effect" are hot air to me.
How can you build a mud house on the sea?[22]

For the one who knows the true nature of
      Existence and Non-Existence,
Being and Non-Being can trouble him.
The one who is free from creation and turns into
      Creator
Isn't bothered by acts and attributes.[23]

The One who was looking at us yesterday
Was either the soul of an angel or the spirit of a
	fairy.
Anyone who lives without seeing His beautiful
	face is dead.
Knowledge of anything without Him comes from
	total ignorance.[24]

It is amazing that the Beloved is contained in my
	heart.
Souls of a thousand bodies fit in this flesh.
One grain grows into thousands of harvests.
Hundreds of universes fit in the eye of a needle.[25]

A Story

Everything I Learned,
I Learned from a Mermaid

Nevit O. Ergin

I first noticed that the distance between two points was getting longer and the mirrors that used to smile at me all those years were not friendly anymore.

Yet I was taking my daily vitamins, exercising regularly, watching my weight. My well-informed friends repeated that if I kept it up, I would stay young, healthy, and strong for a long time, perhaps forever.

Old age and death were for others, not me. I was different.

I worked as a manager of a department store. My family believed I was destined for that job. When I was born, my father bought a cradle from this store. My mother dressed me from the same place when I was a toddler. My first sneakers and jeans also came from there. I became a young salesman, starting out in the bargain basement. I worked every section of every floor, year after year, until I was promoted to manager of the entire store. I took my job seriously. Like a maestro of an orchestra, I demanded absolute control from every section. Then I created harmony and a profitable operation.

I thought this would last forever.

Who assigned me to this job? The Big Boss. He is the only one who hires and fires in this place. He didn't show himself, but He was everywhere all the time. He wasn't responsible to shareholders or any other authority. His justice was different from our justice. We talked about Him all the time, but none of us had ever met or knew Him. This ignorance did not stop the speculation. Some of us thought of Him as a great-grandfather, but most of us thought He was just a Big Boss, one with whom we should get along.

When I received the pink slip I was not disappointed. I knew things were not going well for me lately. My inventory was well exceeding sales, not only cutting profits, but also creating storage problems. I used to wake up in the middle of the night coughing and short of breath. The doctor told me that my heart was failing. I was disappointed more than alarmed. My body had betrayed me. After taking good care of that miserable heart, it couldn't even pump enough blood to let me lie down and sleep.

That brought a new idea to my mind: Death. I realized I had no idea about life. How could I know life if I hadn't died yet? Being born in time and space carries some liabilities such as getting old and sick, eventually leading to death. But if we were going to die, why were we born? I was sure this question had been asked before. But no one has come up with evidence that Creation really took place. Did existence ever exist beyond assumption?[26]

My retirement party came the day after I collapsed in the middle of my office. It was a sad gathering. Participants were dressed in black. Although they had serious expressions on their faces, they were relieved to see me in that position rather than themselves.

I was allowed to stay overnight at the office. After they left, I visited every corner of the store. I used to think these were parts of my body, but I noticed they were already becoming like strangers to me.

I left the store the next morning before anyone arrived at work. I felt like my heart was beating outside of my chest. The air was cool and fresh, and the place was empty, with no shoppers in sight. The shopping center belonged to the stores. I heard the friendly conversation of mannequins through shop windows. A few workers were cleaning the street and watering the plants. A bag lady was sitting, sipping her coffee. I said, "Good morning," as I passed her. She smiled back.

I used to know this place very well, but everything looked strange and new today. I walked aimlessly for hours just looking around, stopping here and there. Then I came to a narrow passage at the edge of the shopping center. There were a few restaurants, flower shops, and a street sign written in French. It read, "Rue de chat qui pêche," or "Fishing Cat Street." It resembled Utrillo's Paris street scenes, windows with green shutters, small balconies with flower boxes full of geraniums and climbing ivies. Next to the sign was a bistro with a gas lamp over the door.

I tried to reach for the doorknob, but someone behind warned, "That's not the door." I turned and came face to face with a small, elderly man. "The door is on the right," he said, pointing to the door with a smile. I was surprised and asked about the door in front of me. "It's only a mural," he said. I pointed to the pots and flowers. He shook his head, "So are they."

The door he opened carried a sign reading, "Authorized Personnel Only." He kept the door open for me, but I hesitated. "I am not an authorized person," I said.

He pulled out a piece of paper from his pocket and looked at it carefully. Then he said, "Yes, here you are." He didn't show me, but apparently my name was there.

We passed through the door into a dimly lit hallway. At the end an open door showed the sea and sky. There were some small houses. "Playhouses, only for display," he explained.

I asked, "Are we outside of the shopping center?"

He looked around and said, "Obviously."

"But where are we?" I asked again. Instead of answering, he

pointed to a sign with the following words inscribed in granite:

"For thousands of years natives who lived on this coastal area disposed of oysters, crab, mussel shells, animal bones, household items, and elderly people into a large pile. Later this was called a shell mound." A tall fence built around the shell mound kept it out of sight.

"How about the mural; who is the painter?" I asked. He was anxious to take me there. There was a small studio next to the wall. One of its doors was open to the shopping center, the other opened to the beach. I saw a tall man with curly grey hair. He was bent over the easel and did not see us. "Master," the man said, "I've brought a new resident here." He turned. The first thing I noticed was the emptiness where his eyes were supposed to be. I tried very hard not to fall in that abyss.

"How could you paint so beautifully without eyes?" I asked.

"Eyes can't see themselves without looking in a mirror.[27] I am making a mirror to see myself," he replied in a soft and deep voice.

I wanted to look at the painting he had just finished. A mermaid held a mirror as she combed her hair. It was colorful, beautiful. I asked "Is she real?"

"Yes," he said. "When a moon is born in your heart you'll see her."

"I'll pray for that," I said.

"Pray for your Essence, not for the divine plane," the painter replied.[28]

"Time to go," said the small man as he held my arm. I was annoyed by his continuous presence and dominance. He realized that and excused himself, leaving me alone.

The sun was setting as I walked along the beach, then night came like an expected guest. Darkness covered the sea and land. I could hear hesitant surf around the rocks.

A faint golden light appeared on the horizon. I sat on the sand watching the new moon rise in its glory. When I started to feel sleepy,

I realized I did not have a place to spend the night. I had forgotten to ask the gentleman who took me around about my accommodations in this strange land.

I started to walk back in the direction I came from. Then I heard a voice: "Where are you going? You were already there."[29]

I turned and looked carefully. There was a woman sitting at the top of the rocks. I walked toward her, and with amazement, I recognized the bag lady. She was mysteriously beautiful. She held a mirror in one hand up to her pale face. She combed her long hair with a gold comb. Her shapely body was covered with scales. "It is me," she said. "Bag lady in morning, mermaid at night. Fish in the water, human in the air."

"What is the difference between you and a human?" I asked.

"The difference between us is that you were immersed in the river; there was water in your six dimensions. How could you see the water?[30] You have to be in the air, then the water. This way you will know the water."

I jumped. "Do you recognize me?" I asked, trying to help her remember me. "Tell me, where am I now? Air or water?"

"Neither one," she answered. "You are between the two realms of Being, intermediate stages between night and day, like dawn and dusk, shore and horizon. Man is not an object, not sand, not water, but a concept, a symbol."[31]

There was a silence. "Look at these shadows," she said, showing me the shadows of trees and rocks under the moonlight. *Our* shadows were nowhere.

I felt chills all over me. She put the mirror in front of my face.

"What do you see?" she asked.

I saw the face of Nothingness.

Questions and Answers about Being and Becoming

Q: Is the Self the same thing as Being?

A: Being is the shadow of our origin, the shadow of our Essence. In other words, being and becoming are all about our existence in this world. Our human perception creates us as separate from the whole, and that's where the trouble starts. Our being and becoming always bothers us, even if we're not conscious about it. We inherited this stain in our being. With our human perception, we are unhappy being here in time. But, we cannot remove this stain all at once. It takes stages. In order to get the stain out, we have to get out of Self through Annihilation.

Q: So there are stages or levels of Annihilation?

A: Yes. Annihilation of Actions, Annihilation of Attributes, and Annihilation of Essence. It takes time and it happens in stages, spontaneously. To reach the first stage takes the longest time, maybe eight or ten or twelve years, depending on the aspirant and their efforts, and it's the most challenging stage to reach.

Q: Would you describe the first stage?

A: As the first stage of this path comes in, daily life is experienced as a daydream. Just like in dreams, one has no concept about time and space; dreams are beyond the limitations of time and space. There is no body, no bodily perception, but there are a lot of images. Rather than body, everything is potentiality, and there is Soul-to-Soul communication. Intellectual questions are dissolved in this stage. Abul Hassan, a Sufi saint who died in 1033, said it beautifully: "I hear, I feel, I speak, but I do not exist."

Q: Is that level of perception what some call the world of spirits?
A: Right now, the world as we see it is all "body" (corporeal). We put everything in terms of the body in order to comprehend it. Even our atoms and particles have to be shaped and weighed for us. This is common and customary. When one reaches the first stage of annihilation (Annihilation of Actions), the world loses this corpuscular sense. In other words, a table is not going to be a table, but a possibility, a potentiality. And that means everything that is done is done through the spirit, through the soul.

We do have a touch of that feeling in our dreams. In that case, there is no body. And, we communicate in a different way. We don't talk to the people in our dreams, at least not in the same way we vocalize language; usually we communicate without talking.

At that level of perception, one has full control of time and space. Time becomes the same; past, present, and future condense and become one. You can be in two places at once. The world becomes a potentiality rather than an existence. A table becomes a possibility rather than an existence.

Q: Once you first experience life as a daydream, how long does the experience last? A minute? An entire part of a day?
A: This state comes and goes at the beginning and becomes permanent at the end. Mevlana says in one of his *rubais* (poems) that a branch full of flowers will eventually turn into a branch full of fruit. At the beginning, the flowers can be smelled and seen and enjoyed, but those flowers eventually turn into fruit and aren't blown around anymore by the wind. It's all a result of annihilation.

Q: And the next stage or level?

A: The next stage is reached a few years after one reaches the Annihilation of Actions. The second stage is called the Annihilation of Attributes, wherein one feels joy and enthusiasm for all things and an overflowing love for Love. This love is pervasive and all-encompassing in the second stage of annihilation.

Q: Can you describe the last stage you mentioned?

A: Annihilation of Essence. Annihilation of Essence is going beyond God. Mr. Shushud said that this path goes from the human to God, through God, and beyond. God is something we created with our human perception. God did not create our Essence. Our Essence goes far beyond our present-day, human perception. God is the Lover; Essence is the Beloved. This can be found in both Mr. Shushud's sayings and in Mevlana's poems.

Q: Is our soul in Nothingness, in non-being?

A: We are totally non-being. Our Being is a dream, an illusion, a mirage. Our Essence is in non-being. Our Being is merely our shadow; there is no substance to it. As Mevlana says, "Existence is a means to reach Absence."

PART 11

On Love

Sayings

Poems

*An Essay: Annihilation and Absence
in Mevlana*

Questions and Answers about Love

Sayings

Hasan Lutfi Shushud

Love could be metaphorical or real, pure love. Metaphorical love is an attraction between individuals or a person to God. Real, pure Love manifests and overwhelms the wayfarer at the level of Annihilation of Attributes. Its source is not from outside, but intrinsic. In this Love, Lover and Beloved are the same. It is spiritual intoxication, inebriation, and the fruit of Annihilation.[1]

A person's love for God is a metaphor. How can one love a God who is unknown?[2]

You are the Beloved, the Almighty is your Lover.[3]

Poems

Mevlana Jalaluddin Rumi

Love came, became the blood in my veins and
    skin.
It emptied me from myself, filled me with the
    Beloved.
Every part of my body is occupied by the Beloved.
Only my name is left to me. He has become the
    rest.[4]

The eye that would see those tulips, roses
Fills this whirling sky with wails, cries.
The drunkenness you can get from one-year-old
    Love
You couldn't get from a thousand-year-old wine.[5]

We are lovers of Love; Muslims are different.
We are small ants; Solomon is different.
Ask from us pale faces, broken hearts.
Silk merchants are different.[6]

In Love, no one is low, no one is high.
Neither sobriety nor drunkenness exists in Love.
There is no protector, no sheikh, no disciple in
    Love,
Only poverty. *Kalenderi* * *rinds*† are in Love.[7]

Resist wearing the cloak of Love as long as you
    can.
But, once you wear it, don't yell, don't cry about
    every trouble.
Keep silent even burning in Love's dress.
At the end, comfort, kindness will arrive for you.[8]

When I heard the word of Love for the first
    time,
I threw my heart and soul under Its feet.
Then, I asked myself if lover and Beloved are two?
They are One. I was cross-eyed.[9]

It appears that Love was borne from me,
But don't believe that.
In fact, I was born from Love.[10]

You are such an ocean of Love that
You have no boundary, no end.
The desire that men and women feel for each
    other
Is only a drop from that ocean.[11]

Only Lovers are human in this world.[12]

---

*A type of dervish who has renounced the world
† A jolly, unconventional, mystical person

I am the proof of Love, I am the verse in the
    Koran.
Read me to the people.
O community of Love, the ladder is in your hands.
Ascend to the sky.[13]

Love is my brother, Love is my father.
My origin, my family is Love.
Love is an eternal relation,
Not blood kinship.[14]

If someone's pulse is not palpitating with Love,
Accept him as a donkey, even if he is Plato.[15]

Live with Love; It is the essence of your soul.
Search for the One who will be yours forever.
Don't call "my soul" anyone who troubles your
    soul.
Call him *haram** even if he brings you your daily
    bread.[16]

Although steps are taken to progress in Love,
Those steps are in a place beyond place.
You see so many beings in this house of illusions
    called world.
Rub your eyes, look at them carefully.
Most of them don't even exist.[17]

Love is such a thing that intoxicates people.
Love is such a thing that gives joy and
    drunkenness.

---

*Religiously forbidden

We are not borne from mothers; Love delivered us.
Hundreds of blessings, hundreds of bravos for
    that mother.[18]

The nicest thing about Love: It is the source of
    troubles.
One is not a lover if he fears troubles.
One has to be brave in the business of Love.
When his soul catches the fire of Love,
He will have to give up his soul.[19]

Love has no beginning, no end. Love is eternal.
Countless people are searching for it.
At the day of resurrection, everyone will be
    kicked off the Divine temple
Except lovers.[20]

Your Love turns every place of worship into a
    tavern.
Your Love sets a bazaar of idols aflame.
Your sorrow's hands, like thieves, reached
    everywhere
And grabbed us in both worlds.[21]

When your Love intends to shed blood,
My soul flies away from body's cage.
If someone has the chance of kissing your sugar
    lips,
He becomes an infidel if he doesn't commit that
    sin.[22]

We discovered the cure in Love:
All the time, we shed our blood to Love.

Love has become our constant friend,
And every moment, Love's breath is with us.[23]

Go, gallop on the ride of Love. Don't be afraid.
Read God's *Ayat* [Covenant] from the Koran of
    Love. Don't be afraid.
When you give up your Self and others,
You become your own Beloved.
Know this well, and don't be afraid.[24]

Since you don't become a lover, go: Weave wool,
    spin thread.
You change hundreds of colors and jobs.
Since there is no Love's wine in your skull,
Go lick the bowls in the kitchen of the wealthy.[25]

The Lover turns around those lonely places
    where the Beloved's tent had been set;
He searches for the traces that have been left.
The devout is busy with prostrations and rosaries
    and cravings for bread.
The Lover runs to the water; he is thirsty. The
    other is hungry.[26]

If the sun had as much pleasure and excitement
    in Love as I do,
It would have never risen. It would be simply
    collapsed.
If all Love were divided between all the lovers in
    the world,
Then one-tenth would go to them; the rest would
    go to me.[27]

Only proof comes from the mind;
The Beloved and friend come from Love.
The former is dirty water. The latter is the water of
    life.
You may ascend to the sky with signs, evidences,
But you won't find the trace of Lovers there.[28]

Your Love has left me exhausted.
I have been worn out, ruined on Your path.
I can neither eat during the day nor sleep at night.
Your love has turned me into my own enemy.[29]

Choose the trouble of Love among all troubles.
I don't know a better way to reach the Beloved.
Don't worry if you don't have wealth and possessions.
Worry if you don't have trouble.[30]

I have been captivated by the drunks and become a
    drunk.
I surrendered to their might and gave up the mind.
I became crazy
In order to be admitted into Love's asylum.[31]

I am in love with Love; Love is with me.
Body is in love with Soul; Soul is with body.
Sometimes I hug Love with my arms;
Sometimes Love hugs me.[32]

O One who lives everyday life,
Shame on you! Why do you live like this?
Don't live without the Love that you should be dying
    for.
If you die for that Love, you become immortal.[33]

An Essay

Annihilation and Absence in Mevlana

Nevit O. Ergin

Mevlana is a great mountain. His lower side is Humanity; His summit is Absence. The difference between the views doesn't come from knowledge or turning or chanting *Hu,* but from Annihilation of Self.

> Absence in Nothingness is my religion,
> Annihilation from existence is what I worship.[34]

> Don't stay idle in this world,
> Be Annihilated, so you can see my face.
> If you want to be like this,
> You have to be like that.
> My business is in Absence.[35]

"Annihilation" and "Absence" are vague, abstract terms for some, but they are the most important Truths for a Sufi. Sufism without Annihilation of Self is nothing but a bird without wings; it never gets off the ground.

As long as the bird stays in the cage,
It always stays under someone's control.[36]

Traditional wisdom, books, discussions, interpretations, and existential monism cannot replace the joy of Ecstatic realization. The most tragic irony of mankind is to leave this world without knowing what we came for and where we are going. Maybe the answers to the questions that bother us the most, such as life, death, God, man, destiny, and the like, are beyond human perception.

Since we are the children of our perception, more so than of Adam and Eve, it is only natural to look for salvation by changing perception. We will never see the true nature of this cosmic illusion, fiction of the mind and memory, this magnificent lie that we call "life," unless we die with the death of Annihilation. This way, one beats chronological death and acquires immortality.

The Divine Truth has never been restricted in any geographical way or constrained in any time span. Anyone who can be born from "Self" could realize this. "Love" is the Divine midwife in this holy birth.

This Love is not metaphorical love, for example between two people or between an individual and God, even though a human has a drop of this ocean when they fall in love.

You are such an ocean of Love that
You have no boundary, no end.
The desire man and woman feel for each other
Is only a drop from that ocean.[37]

Real Love, pure Love, manifests itself as an ecstasy and as different stages of Annihilation.

It appears that Love was born from me,
But don't believe that.
In fact, I was born from that Love.[38]

The one who is not aware of the beginning
Is the one who is first
On the road of Love.[39]

This so-called "Creation" and its product, "Existence," are the major curses that haunt us throughout our lives. Accepting this beginning as a façade, our mind makes us aware that we are all on a death row. The only way we can feel comfortable is if we can deny our mortality.

Seldom do we have the suspicion that maybe our own time- and space-bound perception is what put us in this predicament, that duality is the double vision of the Self.

Love is the only panacea that saves humans:

I was dead, and then came back to life.
I was a cry, then I became a smile.
Love came, and turned me into everlasting glory.[40]

Without question, this journey that we find ourselves on is long, hard, and lonely. As another of Mevlana's sayings goes, "As long as we stay here, God is there. The Soul goes back and forth and stays in the pocket of existence as counterfeit money."

Annihilation happens through:

• Remembrance (*dhikr*)
• Austerity (*riyâdât*)
• Contrition (*inkisâr*)
• And a little help from Fellowship (*şuhba*)*

These have all been tried successfully throughout many past centuries. The footsteps of many sages and saints have mapped this secret land. Mind, reason, and faith are all man's custom-made clothes that humans wear until a certain point in time and usually outgrow and change.

---

*Four practices—Itlak Way (*Way of Liberation*) from Hasan Shushud[41]

Questions and Answers
about Love

Q: Can you talk about the Annihilation of Attributes, of which love is a feature?
A: Yes, and Mevlana is a good example of this. In this stage, an exuberance comes that cannot be controlled. Love becomes our father, our mother, our everything. This kind of love is entirely different from what people believe when they say, "I love God." That's a symbolic love. How can someone love God if they don't know God? We use this term a lot, but we don't know Real Love.

Mevlana was ready to go through to Annihilation of Attributes before he met Shams, but because of Shams, he went through the process quickly. Mevlana and Shams met in 1244 or 1245 CE. Shams left Konya for a while, but in total they were together for two years and a couple of months. His disappearance caused great pain for Mevlana.

Q: Is this love anything like the love between a man and a woman?
A: No. Real Love comes from the inside out. Other love is symbolic love that comes from the outside in. Attaining the level of Annihilation of Attributes is required for Real Love to be experienced.

Q: Are you saying that you cannot reach Love as a state of being?
A: No, not even as a state. Mevlana is a good example of Annihilation of Attributes. His preoccupation with Love can be seen in his poetry.

Q: In what way does explanation change the truth of Love?

A: How do you describe "Love" with words? This kind of feeling needs to be experienced. Truth is not something that can be described and understood. It has to be experienced. Truth is simply too big to fit into words.

Meeting with
Hasan Shushud

►•◄

Klaudio Mihovilovich

*Klaudio Mihovilovich was introduced to Itlak at a Gurdjieff-Bennett
school in 1978. He followed another path for twenty years until
his Beloved died, then returned to the Itlak path in 2011.*

I met Mr. Shushud in June of 1983 when I was thirty-two years old.

A few years earlier, I had attended a nine-month course at Claymont,
a center in West Virginia set up by J. G. Bennett. During that course,
we were introduced to practices from various traditions. One of the
practices was a type of breathing called zikr.

This practice attracted me immediately, and by 1982, I needed to
know more about "the silent zikr," as we used to call it. When I asked
Pierre Elliot, the Director of Studies at Claymont, for more information, he answered, "You must go to the source, Mr. Hasan Shushud."
I wrote to Mr. Shushud, and my request for an audience with him was
approved, so I made arrangements to visit him in Istanbul, Turkey.

During my second visit in January of 1985, Mr. Shushud's health
wasn't good any longer, and when I arrived at his door, his wife told
me to come back in a few days. On my second attempt, I was sent
away again. Finally, on my third attempt, she led me upstairs to his

bedroom. A chair had been set up for me; Mr. Shushud was sitting up in bed.

When I entered the bedroom, a perceivable energy met me. His presence filled the space. My state was instantly affected; it felt like walking from the freezing cold into a room with a warm, wood-burning stove. I perceived Mr. Shushud as a large and radiant individual, with a strong and fluid English-speaking voice. It wasn't until the end of the visit while saying good-bye that it became evident he was a very thin man, of small height.

During our time together, it was never necessary for me to verbalize my questions; he simply answered whatever questions came to my mind. He spoke about his respect for the Prophet Muhammad. In reference to Mevlana he said, "The Pir of this teaching used to live in Macedonia." He also assured me that Pierre Elliot at Claymont could help me.

At one point during my visit, his wife came into the room in an agitated state. She told him in Turkish that a family member was involved in a car accident, in which a child lost his life. To be there, intruding in a sensitive moment like that, made me feel very uneasy. But he calmly continued, and when he described the incident to me in English, he concluded with, "a child has been blessed."

In his final words during my visit he told me to remember him during the breathing practice, and he assured me that he would be there at every breath.

A Story

Two Places at Once

Nevit O. Ergin

When I got there in the early evening, it was later than I had expected to arrive. I was at a well-known resort town next to a big lake. I parked the car close to the hotel where he was staying. Streetlights were lit; autumn leaves scattered around the wet sidewalk as an early autumn rain passed. The remaining part of a torn jazz festival sign was the reminder of past summer days.

The hotel was closed for the season. A few rooms on the first floor were open for some customers. I asked the clerk about Mr. Shushud. He confirmed that Mr. Shushud was there, but to my surprise, he added that there were a few other guests for him as well.

Once I got to his room, I thought of all kinds of excuses to explain my tardiness, but Mr. Shushud said calmly, "I knew you were going to be late."

He was seated by his bed with a few books next to him. There were a few personal items here and there; with the prayer rug, his room was homier than a typical hotel room. "Tomorrow we all will see the house," he said. He was referring to the property where he wanted to set up a school for a small group of people interested in Itlak Yolu. I was one of them, a middle-aged, married professional

174

with children. I wasn't sure if I could commit myself to this lifestyle.

When he noticed my hesitation, he said, "All the streets in this world are dead-end streets. You should die first. Death will find you for sure. Before it comes, why don't you beat death at its own game?" But I thought that death was for others, not for me, at least not yet. Sometime in the very distant future I might fade away in my sleep. He suggested I should retire at age forty or forty-five and spend my time on serious matters. He was in his late fifties and already had realized this lifestyle. "Some friends have accepted my invitation; they are here. You'll meet them tomorrow."

The next day was a sunny, bright day. He introduced me to the rest of the group, seven of them, of all ages and different nationalities. We drove in a small van; it seemed more like we were going on a picnic than on a serious business trip. Mr. Shushud stayed in silence as we watched rolling hills go by for a couple of hours.

"Has anyone seen the underground city around here?" Mr. Shushud asked suddenly. None of us had ever heard about it. He pointed at the area where a few trees were standing and said, "We will take a break if you don't mind."

I sat under the tree. The rest of them went with Mr. Shushud to explore. There was a cool breeze coming through branches. A cricket was singing about last summer.

Suddenly, the sky became red and then white; the ground started shaking. I heard a deafening blast. It did not take long before a mushroom cloud appeared on the horizon.

Fear has its own rule. It's older and stronger than the mind. I ran and found myself at the cave with Mr. Shushud and the others. He was trying to move a big round stone at the entrance. He calmly asked for help, "This door opens and closes only from the inside. It was invented thousands of years ago."

Once the opening was closed, the inside became very dark. No one could see each other, but the fear and helplessness were visible in the frozen silence. After a while, our eyes adjusted to darkness. We noted that light was coming from a ventilation duct, and it helped us to see. Everyone was shaking except Mr. Shushud. His calmness was very comforting at this difficult time. The same questions were shared by everyone, but no one asked, "What has happened?" or "Did Mr. Shushud know beforehand?" No one dared to go outside to find out what had happened. It was a catastrophe on an apocalyptic scale. We all felt lucky to be sheltered in this place. Mr. Shushud had something to do with this good fortune.

"The last civilization started in a cave. The new one may be starting in here," someone said in whispering voice.

He was referring to this place as a cave. It turned out to be a part of a thousand-year-old, well-built underground city that could accommodate several thousand people who were trying to escape from invading terrestrial armies or were hiding from religious persecution. They brought their animals in. They had grain storage places, fresh water wells, air ventilation, toilets, and even a place where they made and stored wines.

I thought the real estate that we were going to see was a pretext. This was the place in his mind. He knew what was going to happen. If he had said, "Get your belongings and follow me," it would have made him a doomsday prophet. But, he was a real Master of Wisdom.

I had known Mr. Shushud for a long time. When I met him in 1955, I was practicing fasting and breathing haphazardly. He put it in a system in Self Annihilation. He introduced me to Itlak Yolu. I left him in 1957 to go overseas. He suggested I should study Mevlana's *Dîvân-i Kebîr,* fast as much as possible, and also do a special kind of breathing. And he reminded me that when the time came, I would go through plenty of suffering.

During the next thirteen years I saw him twice. After that, he came to visit me several times, and I visited him at his home. In the 1960s, the telephone had limited overseas use and the computer did not exist in daily life, thus we communicated by mail. His letters were very special. Not only was his handwriting superb, but their contents were valuable. I saved them carefully.

Some common questions were expressed by someone to Mr. Shushud: "Is this the place you invited us to live?"

Mr. Shushud answered calmly, "Yes."

However, unable to find anyone or anything to blame was frustrating. Even we knew that many lives had been evaporated at Ground Zero. Even the ones who survived had to deal with all kinds of miseries. In this part of Earth, the season would change to winter beneath a starless and endless night. Uncertainty about the present and future makes bomb survivors seem like psychics—the world is not the same anymore.

Someone said, "According to the doomsday clock, we should have had five minutes left."* But there were plenty of signs that our planet was having problems. First, a series of storms hit Earth. One hurricane followed the other, until no names were left to identify them. Earthquakes followed next, shaking the ground violently, and tsunamis washed away coasts without mercy.

But nothing was more damaging than man-made ecological disaster. Equipped with faith in technology, humans had become a "Mighty Predator." The prey was the globe we all lived on. The only cause of this self-destruction was the "Self." The Self has been humanity's biggest curse, "Like a hair in the eye, a thorn in the bottom of the foot." The Self had inherited all kinds of evolutionary forms of perception, the oldest and strongest among them being the "survival instinct." Over time, this trait had degenerated into a most sophisticated predator-prey system.

Reason and Faith had stepped aside with blind eyes, while excessive commercialism, nationalism, and institutional religions paraded around. In the meantime, man's destructive power had increased. In November 1954, Einstein wrote in a letter, "I made one great mistake in my life when I signed the letter to President Roosevelt recommending that the atom bomb be made." It no longer would take an army to

---

*The doomsday clock was created by scientists at the University of Chicago in 1947 to project the likelihood of a global disaster.

produce this kind of calamity. A small group of people would suffice.

The question on every one's mind was what kind of changes in society could prevent something like this from happening? Every social system, religion, and science had been tried, and they all had failed to bring peace and harmony to mankind. Instead, they had divided everyone and brought about this catastrophe.

"When man depletes all his hopes, his frustration reaches into despair. Then God sends a new prophet," an elderly gentleman said softly. "Libraries, universities, computers, they are all gone. Only a prophet, a saint can help us," he added.

We were alone one night; Mr. Shushud was sleeping. I asked a question to everyone, "How do you all know Mr. Shushud?" The answers were either "through friends" or through his book *Masters of Wisdom of Central Asia (Hâcegân Hânedâni)*. One of his sayings explained, "the thirsty go to the fountain, not the other way around." I was curious if he had mentioned fasting or taught zikr (a type of breathing) to them. Everyone said he had, and some still practiced, while others had quit after a while.

We all wanted to know who he was and what he could tell us about who he was.

For the reader of this book, the details of struggle for survival in this environment, which was a long, hard challenge by itself, are omitted in order to concentrate on the content of our discussion with Mr. Shushud. Explanation does to some extent hide the truth.[1] Nevertheless, I have included a summary of what Mr. Shushud shared with us, being as clear as possible. This summary of his words are the sayings that you have found throughout the pages of this book.

He started the discussion by answering our questions about who he was. Many other answers followed over many days and nights. He was calm, patient, and self-confident, and he generously made things clear to most of us.

Mr. Shushud disappeared from our lives one day in just the same way he had come into them. He announced that this was going to be the last night. He was going home, and we should all do the same. It was safe to go out. The next day he was gone.

I stayed in the cave a little longer after everyone left. I told them I was looking for Mr. Shushud, but I knew he was not there. Maybe I was scared to go outside and I was used to this environment. Also, I didn't want to be with anyone.

I heard from somewhere that bomb survivors tend to keep their stories to themselves. I felt physically numb and unable to feel. I couldn't trust anyone; even the world seemed counterfeit. The next day I walked out with the notes I had gathered. Outside it was dark and cold, even though it was supposed to be midday. There was very little green around; everything seemed burned and bare. A cold, scary silence caged me in, like a glass wall around me.

I walked and walked in the direction from which we had all come. I slept when I was exhausted and ate whatever I could find. I drank from here and there, not worrying about contamination. I knew this was an isolated area. When I reached the boundary, I saw all kinds of people. I didn't ask them what had happened, and they didn't ask how I had survived. After a couple of days of observation, I was free again.

I wanted to go to Mr. Shushud's home. It was far away, but I still had questions.

When I knocked, his son opened the door.

"You came late," he said. "His funeral was two weeks ago."

I asked if it was on such and such a day, and he was surprised.

"How did you know?"

"We were all together at night, and he disappeared in the morning." I briefly told him the story.

"Impossible," he said calmly. "The time you're talking about he was with us. He didn't leave this house."

I thanked him and left. On my return, I remembered one of his sayings at our last gathering: "The important thing is while you are here, at the same time you are not."

If this sounds far-fetched, I still have the notes I took from him. I have the proof.

Appendix

More Questions and Answers from along the Path

Q: Are there teachers for someone who wants to be on this path?
A: In Itlak, the teacher or guide is like a lighthouse; they help to light the way. On this path, we say, "Zikr is the teacher." Itlak is about a person changing their own perception to take them to Nothingness, to Absence, to non-being through the Itlak practices of fasting and a different way of breathing. The person on this path has to do this on their own.

Q: Is that why so few are serious about Itlak? They want a human teacher?
A: There are curious people. They try to taste this, and taste that—their spiritual appetite to know things is immense. None of them stays too long on this path. They want to know how to do zikr. They don't care too much about fasting. Once we mention that Itlak is not going to provide a paying future, that there will be pain in their future, they get scared. They want to have good fortune, a good life. If anyone says otherwise, they get discouraged.

Q: Is there an age requirement to start on the path?

A: Anywhere, anytime, any age. The sooner an aspirant starts the better. It is a long walk. The first results may be seen eight to ten or twelve years later, depending on the aspirant and their adherence to the practices.

Q: Are there *any* requirements to start on the path?

A: A person involved with Itlak is someone who is born with the potential to go beyond our earthly perception, someone who is looking for something beyond that. Their religion, nationality, social, and economic status are all irrelevant.

Q: Does faith have a role on this path?

A: No. Faith is religion. There's mind/reasoning, and there's faith. These two are human institutions. Faith doesn't like reasoning; reasoning doesn't like faith. In the West, a kind of non-holy marriage between faith and reason took place during the Renaissance. The West has developed quite a bit through technology, but that isn't universally shared. China and Russia have had some renaissance through communism. Islam has never had a renaissance, and that's causing a lot of trouble.

Q: About how long does it take before real change is accomplished?

A: To reach the first stage of annihilation takes seven or eight, maybe even ten or twelve years. A good beginning may be experienced about a year or two after the aspirant starts fasting, doing zikr, and mentally suffering. Again, it depends on the aspirant. People who suffer intensely reach this change much faster than others. It starts with a kind of déjà vu experience and premonitions, and definitely things start moving into the daydreaming stages. This experience comes and goes at the beginning, then becomes permanent at the end.

Q: Why does it take so long?

A: It's taken billions and billions of years to inherit this perception, and it takes time to crack it. After the first crack, it's easier. Depending on the aspirant, it usually takes seven or eight years to get the first crack, which is into the level of Annihilation of Actions. Reaching Annihilation of Actions is the hardest part. After that, all annihilation is traversing in God (Annihilation of Attributes). To go beyond God is the last stage (Annihilation of Essence), but seldom will anyone have the pleasure and honor of going beyond God. That's called *baka* (Nothingness; permanency).

Q: So it isn't possible to change your habits and behaviors without going through annihilation?
A: Man is in a deep coma of existence because of his perception. Like a silkworm, this perception makes a cocoon with its saliva. Soon it has caged itself there and dies in it. Creation, self, others, time, space, mind, senses, creator, creature, birth, death, the universe—are all products of human perception. Since man's behavior is merely the shadow of his Essence, all attempts to change the direction of his shadow are illusory.

Q: How are you defining the Self?
A: One's perception, human perception. In human perception, there is nothing but Self. Everything humans think, sense, and feel comes from the Self. But before and after the Self, there are unlimited levels of perception, each with a limited awareness of Truth. When we change our perception to another level, our Self disappears.

Q: Does "*fenâ*" mean the same thing as "liberation?"
A: Fenâ is another word for liberation. Liberation is to free oneself from the Self. Both words mean annihilation of the Self. Everything on this path is based on annihilation of the Self. We know annihilation will change our Self from existence to non-existence. Mysticism without annihilation is like a bird without wings; it will stay on the ground. Unfortunately, all the theories of mysticism not based on annihilation are nothing more than literature. Annihilation is doing something to our body. As Mevlana says, "Existence is the means to reach Absence."

Q: How are you defining "Existence?"

A: Existence means our bodily perception. When we change our bodily perception to another perception, we have an entirely different world. Just like in our dreams, we don't see the body any more. We see spirit to spirit; we talk soul to soul.

Q: How are you defining soul?

A: Man is not an object, but a concept like a shore or the horizon. When one reaches the first stage of annihilation (Annihilation of Actions), one understands the soul. Until then, man doesn't understand the body or the soul.

Q: In Mr. Shushud's opening prayer to this book, he says, "Make me obliged to You." What does he mean by the word "obliged"?

A: At the level of human perception, we're fond of politics, health, wealth, and other worldly things. We are obliged to these things. If we were born obliged to God or the divinity or infinity or Absence or whatever word we choose to describe, we'll always look for that, from the day we are born until the day we die. Mr. Shushud would say, "Make me not world-hungry, life-hungry. Make me hungry for You." This theme is repeated again and again by Mevlana. Some poems with this theme are included in the pages of this book. Also I should add, if a person were simply world-hungry, they would not be reading this book.

Q: Quantum physics refers to nothingness. Is this the same "Nothingness" that you refer to?

A: I don't know. I am not a quantum physicist. However, quantum physics may be much closer to what happens when we die than what is proposed by religious and occult people. Our existence swims in Nothingness, because our body is made up of particles. If we look at subatomic particles, they're not here, not there, not alive, not dead. Certainly, they are not within the limits of time and place. This is what a body is—just an infinite number of layers of perception. Our body is temporary, temporary perception. Our Essence is not our body, and it's our Essence that we're trying to reach. Annihilation of Self is the way to do it.

Q: Why does Itlak place so much emphasis on the body?
A: Our body is our only capital. Anything we do is to the body: Fasting, zikr, and suffering mentally are all for the body. We do these to try to find a non-dualistic perception. Everything we do is for the purpose of dying before our death.

Q: How exactly does fasting work to change the body?
A: Our body needs a certain amount of food energy and oxygen. Manipulating the input of food and oxygen certainly changes our perception. Our blood goes from alkalosis to acidosis, and this has a tremendous effect on our perception if it is done for a period of time. Eventually, we can see things are changing.

Cutting back on food intake must be done voluntarily. An aspirant chooses not to eat, even though they may be tempted at every turn because there is plenty of food around them all the time. It's also important to note that one has to have fasting *and* feasting. (The taste of food will always be appreciated.)

Q: Does meditation have any role in Itlak? Is fasting a type of meditation?
A: Meditation is a fairly loose term that has been abused over the years. People say they're meditating, but we have no evidence of what they're really doing. They could be thinking about anything. On the other hand, when one fasts, it affects all of the cells in the body, which eventually affects one's brain, one's perception. That's the substantial difference between meditation and fasting.

Q: When you do zikr, do you silently repeat a word or focus on anything in particular?

A: Holding the breath is the most important part of zikr. When doing it, the focus can be on anything. Any word or anything else can be repeated. But it's not something that we do.

Q: Is there a relationship between fasting and zikr?

A: You start with fasting. Fasting is a little unpalatable for a lot of people. They're afraid to miss breakfast. Actually, if we miss breakfast, we don't feel hungry at lunch. Fasting becomes intensified if we don't break the fast on the same day and let it go another day or even another. We don't feel hungry the next day at all.

But again, fasting goes with zikr. Zikr goes with fasting. Seldom does an aspirant do just one or the other. The two practices bring contrition, suffering. It doesn't take very long. Suffering comes in the proper time.

About the Authors

Mevlana Jalaluddin Rumi,
Hasan Lutfi Shushud, and Nevit O. Ergin

►•◄

MEVLANA JALALUDDIN RUMI

When an Afghan, Iranian, and Turk get together, each one endlessly argues that Mevlana belongs to their own country, which is understandable. They are all right—to some extent.

He was born in a country we call Afghanistan now (in the north); he recited almost all of his poems in thirteenth-century Farsi; and he lived most of his life and died in 1273 in Anatolia, the old land of Rome, present-day Turkey.

The East calls him Mevlana—our Master. The West calls him Rumi—the land he lived in.

His full name is Mevlana Jalaluddin Rumi. In spite of patriotic fervor, almost everyone accepts that the treasure of Mevlana Jalaluddin Rumi cannot fit in any one country's boundary.

He belongs to the whole of humanity.

Seldom has a man started as a man like he was, ended up so close to the Almighty, and related this account in such an eloquent and abundant way to others. None of the great writers, poets, or philosophers in history could match his style and sincerity, neither in quality or quantity.

He was certainly much larger than life. But at the same time, he was very close to mankind, without any religious or racial boundary.

Mevlana Jalaluddin is like an infinitely large umbrella covering all we have and beyond.

Who was he? Most reference books say something along the lines of: "A Persian mystic and poet who was born in 1207 and died in 1273."

How about his birth date? Some of the events registered in the last part of the twelfth and early thirteenth century chronicles cast some doubt about the validity of his 1207 birth date.

In one of his works, *Fih-i Mafih,* Mevlana talks about the siege of Semerkant, which took place in 1207. Also of note is the following poem from his *Divan-i Kebir:*[1]

I have been freed from chains once more.
Once more I jumped out of this trap,
Out of these bonds which bind the weak.

Fate is like an old man
With a hunch on his back,
Full of spells and treachery.
I took refuge in the kingdom of youth,
Escaped from that old man.

I have run day and night;
Flew day and night.
Ask the sky to understand
How I flew off into space like an arrow.

Why should I be afraid of grief and sorrow?
I am a friend and acquaintance with death.
Why should I worry about the doorkeeper?
I have escaped, am saved from the master.

Forty-year-old mind submerged me in thought.
I became prey in my sixty-second year.

I was hunted, then I was freed
From thought and measures.

With God's foreordaining,
All the people became blind and deaf.
Because of the greatness of fate,
I am exempt from that fate.

Fruit is involved with
The shell outside and the seed inside.
I am free from that skin and seed, like a fig.

It is harmful to delay some things,
And the devil makes you hurry others.
My heart is saved from delays and hurry.

First I was fed by blood, then milk.
Then milk became food for me instead of blood.
When my wisdom teeth came in, I was weaned
    from milk.

I ran after bread with a pack of lies for some time.
Since God gave me food, I am free from lies and
    deceit.

Be silent, silent. Don't give all the details.
I talk interpretation.
I am free from the desire for garlic.

Unless Mevlana, at the age of sixty-two, was hunted by someone
other than Shams, unless Mevlana made up being at Semerkant when
the city was seized by Khwarzms, then we may still accept his birth date
as 1207. But who is the one who gave us this date?

My first birth was long past now.
I am born from Love.
I am more than myself.
This is my second birth.[2]

He never mentioned any birth date; neither did his son Sultan Veled. Feriddun Sipahsaler was the first to mention September 30, 1207 as his birth date. When Ahmet Eflaki repeated it in the *Menakubu Arifin*, this date became official from that point on. Eflaki, who died in 1360, was a student of Mevlana's grandson Ulu Arif Celebi.

Mevlana describes himself as follows:

I am neither Christian nor Jew,
Neither Persian nor Moslem,
Neither from land, nor from water.
My place is without place,
My trace is what is, without trace.
I put aside duality.
I have seen two worlds in one.
He is the first, He is the last,
He is within, He is without.[3]

He certainly rejected the ideas that confine him in any particular location or religion:

I am concealed, secret sometimes;
Sometimes I appear and become obvious.
Sometimes I am Muslim,
Sometimes I am in the faith of Moses.
Sometimes I am Christian.
In order to be a model to everyone,
I manifest differently in every time.[4]

He also rejects the cycle of day and night:

Day brings your fights, your struggles.
There is love in the head of the evening.
My business is not the business of day and night.
How could these two lame donkeys carry my load?[5]

In the following quatrain, or rubai, he describes himself:

They had experts appraise
My turban, my robe, my head.
They gave the price as less than a dirham (penny).
Haven't you heard my name in the world?
I have been annihilated.
I am nothing.
I am Absent.[6]

"Annihilation, Nothingness, Absence" . . . when one searches for him, he is pointing where to look. Certainly it isn't in his robe or turban.

There is an inherent danger in Rumi's poems. They dazzle the eyes with their poetic beauty, so that one cannot see their saintly, prophetic meaning.

The price that he is asking to understand him is definitely not cheap. But who expects immortality to be cheap?

O one who wants to smell my fragrance,
You must die first.
Don't look for me
When you are alive.[7]

The death he refers to here is obviously not chronological death; it is the salvation from the dungeon of existence. It is also not an intellectual concept, but the direct experience of immortality (as described by Mr. Hasan Shushud). Mevlana is the Prince of Absence. He is God's Lover. Calling him a poet (it doesn't matter how great a poet) is a big discredit to him.

> O sultan of eternity,
> I am free from gazelles, from verses.
> Tell the rhyme, the meter,
> That the torrent should wash them out.
> The only thing a poet could do
> Is scratch the surface.[8]

> I am not a poet.
> My sustenance doesn't come from poetry.
> Also, I don't talk much about virtue.
> My virtue, my talent is a glass of Love.
> I drink that only from the hand of the Beloved,
> Not from anyone else.[9]

Mevlana did not come from any particular (Sufi) school. His first teacher was his father, Muhammed Bahaeddin Veled (1151–1231). After his father's death, a student of his father's, Burhaneddin Muhakkik (who died in 1241) became Mevlana's teacher.

Mevlana was a Muslim theologian but he did not originate from any Sufi sect himself; he took over his father's religious school. The Mevlevi movement started many years after his death. We would most likely never know him if he hadn't met Shams on one Saturday in the fall—October or November 24, 1244.

His spiritual life started immediately after that.

It is very difficult to call him a mystic, in the traditional sense at least. But universally he was one of the best.

> I am the pure-hearted Sufi
> At the convent of the Universe,
> Not one who wears a woolen cloak.[10]

HASAN LUTFI SHUSHUD

Hasan Shushud was actually born in Odemis, a town in the west of Anatolia near Izmir on June 6, 1902, although his birth certificate indicates a birthplace of Karaferya, which is in Macedonia, with a date of birth of June 6, 1903. His family had lived in Konya until Ottoman Sultan Murad II conquered Macedonia. At that time, they were relocated to Macedonia.

His father was Defterdar, a financial administrator. Until Mr. Shushud was seventeen years old, he attended St. Michael High School and foreign language schools where he became fluent in French and German and adequate in English. He married a distant cousin, Nuriye Hanim. They had three children: one girl and two boys. He initially worked as a teacher and then worked at various banks for most of his professional life.

Mr. Shushud stated that his spiritual life began in 1917 and benefited from two or three guides in different places.

He published *Hâcegân Hânedâni* in Istanbul in 1958, as well as a book of his aphorisms, *Fakir Sözleri*. *Hâcegân Hânedâni* was translated

Hasan Shushud in the mid-1930s

into English in 1983 under the name of *Masters of Wisdom of Central Asia*.
He died on January 1, 1988.

NEVIT O. ERGIN

Some of us are born restless, like a misfit; often not satisfied by the offers
of religion, science, and philosophy, we live this life as a houseless home cat.

Some of us don't want the comfort of conformity and tradition, so
we accept the quest for truth as an individual journey, like the process
of one's own death.

"Self" is the greatest enemy in this journey. Self is a hair in the eye,
a thorn in the bottom of the soul's foot. Unless it is removed, no one
can see or walk. There won't be peace on Earth until everyone wages
war against the Self. When they become the martyr of their selves, then
they conquer Eternity.

Some of us believe Creation has never taken place, that humanity is the child of perception, and the universe is an hallucination. We
are stuck in this world like a silkworm caged in its self-made cocoon.
Seldom do we have the suspicion that our limited perception put us in
this predicament. Some of us believe there was no Beginning, and that
there is no End. Man has never been born, so they never die.

Some of us also believe the answers to most of man's questions (such
as those about God, Man, Life, and Death) are beyond man's time- and
space-bound perception. The great mystery is always in man's realm. No
one could franchise it, since search for Truth is the inborn nostalgia in
everyone, anytime and any place.

I am one of those restless misfits who became prey to Mevlana sixty
years ago. I found this world in 1928, and I have been trying to get rid
of it since then before it gets rid of me. . . .

Notes

In many cases the author has cited numerous sources for one particular citation, due to conflicting scholarship as regards original material. Readers are encouraged to avail themselves of various sources to arrive at their own conclusions.

PART 1. ON SAINTHOOD AND PROPHETHOOD

1. Shushud, *Hâcegân Hânedâni,* 155; Shushud, *Masters of Wisdom of Central Asia,* 149.

2. Shushud, *Hâcegân Hânedâni,* 155; Shushud, *Masters of Wisdom of Central Asia,* 150.

3. Yonsel, *Tasavvufundan Derinliklerinde Bir Gezinti,* 8.

4. Shushud, *Hâcegân Hânedâni,* 155; Shushud, *Masters of Wisdom of Central Asia,* 15.

5. Shushud, *Hâcegân Hânedâni,* 155; Shushud, *Masters of Wisdom of Central Asia,* 150.

6. Ibid.

7. Yonsel, *Tasavvufundan Derinliklerinde Bir Gezinti,* 27.

8. Can, *Hz. Mevlânâ'nin Rubâîleri,* v. 1006; Ergin, *Mevlânâ Celâleddin Rubâîler,* 233; Forûzânfar (ed.), *Kulliyât-é snams yâ dîwân-é kabîr-e mawlânâ jalâluddîn Muhammad mashhûr ba-mawlawî,* v. 898; Gölpinarli, *Mevlânâ Celâleddin, Rubâîler,* 119, v. 14.

194

PART 2. ON ITLAK, PATH OF ANNIHILATION

1. Shushud, *Hâcegân Hânedâni*, 160; Shushud, *Masters of Wisdom of Central Asia*, 153.

2. Yonsel, *Tasavvufundan Derinliklerinde Bir Gezinti*, 21.

3. Shushud, *Masters of Wisdom of Central Asia*, 155.

4. Shushud, *Hâcegân Hânedâni*, 160; Shushud, *Masters of Wisdom of Central Asia*, 145.

5. Yonsel, *Tasavvufundan Derinliklerinde Bir Gezinti*, 57.

6. Ibid., 53.

7. Ibid., 42.

8. Shushud, *Hâcegân Hânedâni*, 145; Shushud, *Masters of Wisdom of Central Asia*, 157.

9. Yonsel, *Tasavvufundan Derinliklerinde Bir Gezinti*, 61.

10. Shushud, *Hâcegân Hânedâni*, 165; Shushud, *Masters of Wisdom of Central Asia*, 158.

11. Yonsel, *Tasavvufundan Derinliklerinde Bir Gezinti*, 22.

12. Ibid., 11.

13. Shushud, *Hâcegân Hânedâni*, 165; Shushud, *Masters of Wisdom of Central Asia*, 158.

14. Ibid.

15. Yonsel, *Tasavvufundan Derinliklerinde Bir Gezinti*, 21.

16. Shushud, *Hâcegân Hânedâni*, 165; Shushud, *Masters of Wisdom of Central Asia*, 158.

17. Shushud, *Hâcegân Hânedâni*, 161; Shushud, *Masters of Wisdom of Central Asia*, 155.

18. Yonsel, *Tasavvufundan Derinliklerinde Bir Gezinti*, 35.

19. Can, *Hz. Mevlânâ'nin Rubâîleri*, v. 790; Ergin, *Mevlânâ Celâleddin Rubâîler*, 143; Forûzânfar (ed.), *Kulliyât-é snams yâ dîwân-é kabîr-e mawlânâ jalâluddîn Muhammad mashhûr ba-mawlawî*, v. 737; Gölpinarli, *Dîvân-i Kebîr Mevlânâ Celâleddin*, 70, v. 24.

20. Can, *Hz. Mevlânâ'nin Rubâîleri*, v. 409; Ergin, *Mevlânâ Celâleddin Rubâîler*, 90; Forûzânfar (ed.), *Kulliyât-é snams yâ dîwân-é kabîr-e mawlânâ jalâluddîn Muhammad mashhûr ba-mawlawî*, v. 391; Gölpinarli, *Dîvân-i Kebîr Mevlânâ Celâleddin*, 61, v. 275.

21. Can, *Hz. Mevlânâ'nin Rubâîleri,* v. 881; Ergin, *Mevlânâ Celâleddin Rubâîler,* 203; Forûzânfar (ed.), *Kulliyât-é snams yâ dîwân-é kabîr-e mawlânâ jalâluddîn Muhammad mashhûr ba-mawlawî,* v. 829; Gölpinarli, *Dîvân-i Kebîr Mevlânâ Celâleddin,* 92, v. 217.

22. Can, *Hz. Mevlânâ'nin Rubâîleri,* v. 543; Ergin, *Mevlânâ Celâleddin Rubâîler,* 220; Forûzânfar (ed.), *Kulliyât-é snams yâ dîwân-é kabîr-e mawlânâ jalâluddîn Muhammad mashhûr ba-mawlawî,* v. 488; Gölpinarli, *Dîvân-i Kebîr Mevlânâ Celâleddin,* 95, v. 247.

23. Can, *Hz. Mevlânâ'nin Rubâîleri,* v. 306; Ergin, *Mevlânâ Celâleddin Rubâîler,* 80; Forûzânfar (ed.), *Kulliyât-é snams yâ dîwân-é kabîr-e mawlânâ jalâluddîn Muhammad mashhûr ba-mawlawî,* v. 288; Gölpinarli, *Mevlânâ Celâleddin, Rubâîler,* T38, v. 87.

24. Can, *Hz. Mevlânâ'nin Rubâîleri,* v. 671; Ergin, *Mevlânâ Celâleddin Rubâîler,* 151; Forûzânfar (ed.), *Kulliyât-é snams yâ dîwân-é kabîr-e mawlânâ jalâluddîn Muhammad mashhûr ba-mawlawî,* v. 617; Gölpinarli, *Mevlânâ Celâleddin, Rubâîler,* 267, v. 122.

25. Can, *Hz. Mevlânâ'nin Rubâîleri,* v. 863; Ergin, *Mevlânâ Celâleddin Rubâîler,* 203; Forûzânfar (ed.), *Kulliyât-é snams yâ dîwân-é kabîr-e mawlânâ jalâluddîn Muhammad mashhûr ba-mawlawî,* v. 811; Gölpinarli, *Mevlânâ Celâleddin, Rubâîler,* D91, v. 216.

26. Can, *Hz. Mevlânâ'nin Rubâîleri,* v. 795; Ergin, *Mevlânâ Celâleddin Rubâîler,* 205; Forûzânfar (ed.), *Kulliyât-é snams yâ dîwân-é kabîr-e mawlânâ jalâluddîn Muhammad mashhûr ba-mawlawî,* v. 742; Gölpinarli, *Mevlânâ Celâleddin, Rubâîler,* D73, v. 53.

27. Can, *Hz. Mevlânâ'nin Rubâîleri,* v. 568; Ergin, *Mevlânâ Celâleddin Rubâîler,* 207; Forûzânfar (ed.), *Kulliyât-é snams yâ dîwân-é kabîr-e mawlânâ jalâluddîn Muhammad mashhûr ba-mawlawî,* v. 513; Gölpinarli, *Mevlânâ Celâleddin, Rubâîler,* D93, v. 223.

28. Can, *Hz. Mevlânâ'nin Rubâîleri,* v. 1495; Ergin, *Mevlânâ Celâleddin Rubâîler,* 331; Forûzânfar (ed.), *Kulliyât-é snams yâ dîwân-é kabîr-e mawlânâ jalâluddîn Muhammad mashhûr ba-mawlawî,* v. 1359; Gölpinarli, *Mevlânâ Celâleddin, Rubâîler,* M154, v. 129.

29. Can, *Hz. Mevlânâ'nin Rubâîleri,* v. 1605; Ergin, *Mevlânâ Celâleddin Rubâîler,* 335; Forûzânfar (ed.), *Kulliyât-é snams yâ dîwân-é kabîr-e mawlânâ jalâluddîn Muhammad mashhûr ba-mawlawî,* v. 1442; Gölpinarli, *Mevlânâ Celâleddin, Rubâîler,* N169, v. 18.

30. Can, *Hz. Mevlânâ'nin Rubâîleri,* v. 1555; Ergin, *Mevlânâ Celâleddin*

Notes 197

Rubâîler, 340; Forûzânfar (ed.), *Kulliyât-é snams yâ dîwân-é kabîr-e mawlânâ jalâluddîn Muhammad mashhûr ba-mawlawî,* v. 1392; Gölpinarli, *Mevlânâ Celâleddin, Rubâîler,* N170, v. 32.

31. Can, *Hz. Mevlânâ'nin Rubâîleri,* v. 1806; Ergin, *Mevlânâ Celâleddin Rubâîler,* 392; Forûzânfar (ed.), *Kulliyât-é snams yâ dîwân-é kabîr-e mawlânâ jalâluddîn Muhammad mashhûr ba-mawlawî,* v. 1621; Gölpinarli, *Mevlânâ Celâleddin, Rubâîler,* H189, v. 71.

32. Can, *Hz. Mevlânâ'nin Rubâîleri,* v. 1807; Ergin, *Mevlânâ Celâleddin Rubâîler,* 393; Forûzânfar (ed.), *Kulliyât-é snams yâ dîwân-é kabîr-e mawlânâ jalâluddîn Muhammad mashhûr ba-mawlawî,* v. 1622; Gölpinarli, *Mevlânâ Celâleddin, Rubâîler,* H189, v. 74.

33. Can, *Hz. Mevlânâ'nin Rubâîleri,* v. 2122; Ergin, *Mevlânâ Celâleddin Rubâîler,* 403; Forûzânfar (ed.), *Kulliyât-é snams yâ dîwân-é kabîr-e mawlânâ jalâluddîn Muhammad mashhûr ba-mawlawî,* v. 1930; Gölpinarli, *Mevlânâ Celâleddin, Rubâîler,* Y199, v. 16.

34. Can, *Hz. Mevlânâ'nin Rubâîleri,* v. 2121; Ergin, *Mevlânâ Celâleddin Rubâîler,* 442; Forûzânfar (ed.), *Kulliyât-é snams yâ dîwân-é kabîr-e mawlânâ jalâluddîn Muhammad mashhûr ba-mawlawî,* v. 1929; Gölpinarli, *Mevlânâ Celâleddin, Rubâîler,* Y207, v. 85.

35. Can, *Hz. Mevlânâ'nin Rubâîleri,* v. 1585; Ergin, *Mevlânâ Celâleddin Rubâîler,* 336; Forûzânfar (ed.), *Kulliyât-é snams yâ dîwân-é kabîr-e mawlânâ jalâluddîn Muhammad mashhûr ba-mawlawî,* v. 1422; Gölpinarli, *Mevlânâ Celâleddin, Rubâîler,* N170, v. 19.

36. Can, *Hz. Mevlânâ'nin Rubâîleri,* v. 1614; Ergin, *Mevlânâ Celâleddin Rubâîler,* 338; Forûzânfar (ed.), *Kulliyât-é snams yâ dîwân-é kabîr-e mawlânâ jalâluddîn Muhammad mashhûr ba-mawlawî,* v. 1451; Gölpinarli, *Mevlânâ Celâleddin, Rubâîler,* N170, v. 26.

37. Shushud, personal communication recorded in 1963.

PART 3. ON HUMANKIND

1. Shushud, *Hâcegân Hânedâni,* 136; Shushud, *Masters of Wisdom of Central Asia,* 131.

2. Yonsel, *Tasavvfundan Derînliklerinde Bir Gezînti,* 41.

3. Ibid., 66.

4. Shushud, *Hâcegân Hânedâni,* 140; Shushud, *Masters of Wisdom of Central Asia,* 134.

5. Shushud, *Hâcegân Hânedâni*, 149; Shushud, *Masters of Wisdom of Central Asia*, 144.

6. Ibid.

7. Yonsel, *Tasavvfundan Derinliklerinde Bir Gezinti*, 60.

8. Ibid., 31.

9. Ibid.

10. Ibid., 41.

11. Ibid., 32.

12. Ibid., 11.

13. Ibid., 32.

14. Ibid., 37.

15. Ibid., 47.

16. Ibid., 5.

17. Ibid., 45.

18. Ibid., 53.

19. Ibid., 59.

20. Ibid., 60.

21. Ibid.

22. Ibid., 62.

23. Ibid., 69.

24. Ibid., 43.

25. Gölpinarli, *Dîvân-i Kebîr Mevlânâ Celâleddin*.

26. Can, *Hz. Mevlânâ'nin Rubâîleri*, v. 183; Ergin, *Mevlânâ Celâleddin Rubâîler*, 109; Forûzânfar (ed.), *Kulliyât-é snams yâ dîwân-é kabîr-e mawlânâ jalâluddîn Muhammad mashhûr ba-mawlawî*, v. 165; Gölpinarli, *Dîvân-i Kebîr Mevlânâ Celâleddin*, 46, v. 153.

27. Can, *Hz. Mevlânâ'nin Rubâîleri*, v. 1975; Ergin, *Mevlânâ Celâleddin Rubâîler*, 431; Forûzânfar (ed.), *Kulliyât-é snams yâ dîwân-é kabîr-e mawlânâ jalâluddîn Muhammad mashhûr ba-mawlawî*, v. 1782; Gölpinarli, *Dîvân-i Kebîr Mevlânâ Celâleddin*, 205, v. 66.

28. Can, *Hz. Mevlânâ'nin Rubâîleri*, v. 1386; Forûzânfar (ed.), *Kulliyât-é snams yâ dîwân-é kabîr-e mawlânâ jalâluddîn Muhammad mashhûr ba-mawlawî*, v. 1249; Gölpinarli, *Dîvân-i Kebîr Mevlânâ Celâleddin*, 150, v. 94.

29. Can, *Hz. Mevlânâ'nin Rubâîleri*, v. 1791; Forûzânfar (ed.), *Kulliyât-é snams yâ dîwân-é kabîr-e mawlânâ jalâluddîn Muhammad mashhûr ba-mawlawî*, v. 1606; Gölpinarli, *Dîvân-i Kebîr Mevlânâ Celâleddin*, 185, v. 44.

30. Can, *Hz. Mevlânâ'nin Rubâîleri*, v. 2113; Ergin, *Mevlânâ Celâleddin Rubâîler*, 421; Forûzânfar (ed.), *Kulliyât-é snams yâ dîwân-é kabîr-e mawlânâ jalâluddîn Muhammad mashhûr ba-mawlawî*, v. 1921; Gölpinarli, *Dîvân-i Kebîr Mevlânâ Celâleddin*, 200, v. 27.

31. Can, *Hz. Mevlânâ'nin Rubâîleri*, v. 515; Ergin, *Mevlânâ Celâleddin Rubâîler*, 148; Forûzânfar (ed.), *Kulliyât-é snams yâ dîwân-é kabîr-e mawlânâ jalâluddîn Muhammad mashhûr ba-mawlawî*, v. 460; Gölpinarli, *Dîvân-i Kebîr Mevlânâ Celâleddin*, 105, v. 326.

32. Can, *Hz. Mevlânâ'nin Rubâîleri*, v. 1721; Ergin, *Mevlânâ Celâleddin Rubâîler*, 362; Forûzânfar (ed.), *Kulliyât-é snams yâ dîwân-é kabîr-e mawlânâ jalâluddîn Muhammad mashhûr ba-mawlawî*, v. 1545; Gölpinarli, *Dîvân-i Kebîr Mevlânâ Celâleddin*,193, v. 33.

33. Ergin, *Dîvân-i Kebîr of Mevlânâ Celâleddin Rumi*, Meter8a, 124, v. 592.

34. Can, *Hz. Mevlânâ'nin Rubâîleri*, v. 2122; Ergin, *Mevlânâ Celâleddin Rubâîler*, 403; Forûzânfar (ed.), *Kulliyât-é snams yâ dîwân-é kabîr-e mawlânâ jalâluddîn Muhammad mashhûr ba-mawlawî*, v. 1930; Gölpinarli, *Dîvân-i Kebîr Mevlânâ Celâleddin*, 199, v. 16.

35. Can, *Hz. Mevlânâ'nin Rubâîleri*, v. 215; Ergin, *Mevlânâ Celâleddin Rubâîler*, 80; Forûzânfar (ed.), *Kulliyât-é snams yâ dîwân-é kabîr-e mawlânâ jalâluddîn Muhammad mashhûr ba-mawlawî*, v. 197; Gölpinarli, *Mevlânâ Celâleddin, Rubâîler*, 327, v. 252.

36. Can, *Hz. Mevlânâ'nin Rubâîleri*, v. 718; Ergin, *Mevlânâ Celâleddin Rubâîler*, 148; Forûzânfar (ed.), *Kulliyât-é snams yâ dîwân-é kabîr-e mawlânâ jalâluddîn Muhammad mashhûr ba-mawlawî*, v. 644; Gölpinarli, *Mevlânâ Celâleddin, Rubâîler*, D69 v. 19.

37. Can, *Hz. Mevlânâ'nin Rubâîleri*, v. 783; Ergin, *Mevlânâ Celâleddin Rubâîler*, 194; Forûzânfar (ed.), *Kulliyât-é snams yâ dîwân-é kabîr-e mawlânâ jalâluddîn Muhammad mashhûr ba-mawlawî*, v. 730; Gölpinarli, *Mevlânâ Celâleddin, Rubâîler*, D72, v. 47.

38. Can, *Hz. Mevlânâ'nin Rubâîleri*, v. 801; Ergin, *Mevlânâ Celâleddin Rubâîler*, 202; Forûzânfar (ed.), *Kulliyât-é snams yâ dîwân-é kabîr-e mawlânâ jalâluddîn Muhammad mashhûr ba-mawlawî*, v. 748; Gölpinarli, *Mevlânâ Celâleddin, Rubâîler*, D99, v. 282.

39. Can, *Hz. Mevlânâ'nin Rubâîleri*, v. 577; Ergin, *Mevlânâ Celâleddin*

Rubâîler, 207; Forûzânfar (ed.), *Kulliyât-é snams yâ dîwân-é kabîr-e mawlânâ jalâluddîn Muhammad mashhûr ba-mawlawî,* v. 522; Gölpinarli, *Mevlânâ Celâleddin, Rubâîler,* D114, v. 406.

40. Can, *Hz. Mevlânâ'nin Rubâîleri,* v. 726; Ergin, *Mevlânâ Celâleddin Rubâîler,* 213; Forûzânfar (ed.), *Kulliyât-é snams yâ dîwân-é kabîr-e mawlânâ jalâluddîn Muhammad mashhûr ba-mawlawî,* v. 672; Gölpinarli, *Mevlânâ Celâleddin, Rubâîler,* D74, v. 60.

41. Can, *Hz. Mevlânâ'nin Rubâîleri,* v. 1024; Ergin, *Mevlânâ Celâleddin Rubâîler,* 234; Forûzânfar (ed.), *Kulliyât-é snams yâ dîwân-é kabîr-e mawlânâ jalâluddîn Muhammad mashhûr ba-mawlawî,* v. 916; Gölpinarli, *Mevlânâ Celâleddin, Rubâîler,* D120, v. 121.

42. Can, *Hz. Mevlânâ'nin Rubâîleri,* v. 1728; Ergin, *Mevlânâ Celâleddin Rubâîler,* 366; Forûzânfar (ed.), *Kulliyât-é snams yâ dîwân-é kabîr-e mawlânâ jalâluddîn Muhammad mashhûr ba-mawlawî,* v. 1552; Gölpinarli, *Mevlânâ Celâleddin, Rubâîler,* V190, v. 8.

43. Can, *Hz. Mevlânâ'nin Rubâîleri,* v. 1746; Ergin, *Mevlânâ Celâleddin Rubâîler,* 372; Forûzânfar (ed.), *Kulliyât-é snams yâ dîwân-é kabîr-e mawlânâ jalâluddîn Muhammad mashhûr ba-mawlawî,* v. 1570; Gölpinarli, *Mevlânâ Celâleddin, Rubâîler,* V196, v. 56.

44. Can, *Hz. Mevlânâ'nin Rubâîleri,* v. 2036; Ergin, *Mevlânâ Celâleddin Rubâîler,* 422; Forûzânfar (ed.), *Kulliyât-é snams yâ dîwân-é kabîr-e mawlânâ jalâluddîn Muhammad mashhûr ba-mawlawî,* v. 1843; Gölpinarli, *Mevlânâ Celâleddin, Rubâîler,* Y216, v. 181.

45. Can, *Hz. Mevlânâ'nin Rubâîleri,* v. 2049; Ergin, *Mevlânâ Celâleddin Rubâîler,* 440; Forûzânfar (ed.), *Kulliyât-é snams yâ dîwân-é kabîr-e mawlânâ jalâluddîn Muhammad mashhûr ba-mawlawî,* v. 1856; Gölpinarli, *Mevlânâ Celâleddin, Rubâîler,* Y207, v. 88.

46. Can, *Hz. Mevlânâ'nin Rubâîleri,* v. 2097; Ergin, *Mevlânâ Celâleddin Rubâîler,* 470; Forûzânfar (ed.), *Kulliyât-é snams yâ dîwân-é kabîr-e mawlânâ jalâluddîn Muhammad mashhûr ba-mawlawî,* v. 1905; Gölpinarli, *Mevlânâ Celâleddin, Rubâîler,* Y226, v. 244.

PART 4. ON GOD

1. Shushud, *Hâcegân Hânedâni,* 141; Shushud, *Masters of Wisdom of Central Asia,* 137.

2. Yonsel, *Tasavvfundan Derinliklerinde Bir Gezinti,* 23.

3. Ibid., 23.

4. Ibid.

5. Ibid., 47.

6. Ibid., 52.

7. Ibid., 35.

8. Ergin, *Dîvân-i Kebîr of Mevlânâ Celâleddin Rumi, Meter 1*, 296, v. 1551.

9. Can, *Hz. Mevlânâ'nin Rubâîleri*, v. 1733; Forûzânfar (ed.), *Kulliyât-é snams yâ dîwân-é kabîr-e mawlânâ jalâluddîn Muhammad mashhûr ba-mawlawî*, v. 1557; Gölpinarli, *Dîvân-i Kebîr Mevlânâ Celâleddin*, 191, v. 15.

10. Can, *Hz. Mevlânâ'nin Rubâîleri*, v. 1814; Forûzânfar (ed.), *Kulliyât-é snams yâ dîwân-é kabîr-e mawlânâ jalâluddîn Muhammad mashhûr ba-mawlawî*, v. 1629; Gölpinarli, *Dîvân-i Kebîr Mevlânâ Celâleddin*, 182, v. 20.

11. Can, *Hz. Mevlânâ'nin Rubâîleri*, v. 151; Ergin, *Mevlânâ Celâleddin Rubâîler*, 104; Forûzânfar (ed.), *Kulliyât-é snams yâ dîwân-é kabîr-e mawlânâ jalâluddîn Muhammad mashhûr ba-mawlawî*, v. 133; Gölpinarli, *Dîvân-i Kebîr Mevlânâ Celâleddin*, 64, v. 301.

12. Can, *Hz. Mevlânâ'nin Rubâîleri*, v. 637; Ergin, *Mevlânâ Celâleddin Rubâîler*, 209; Forûzânfar (ed.), *Kulliyât-é snams yâ dîwân-é kabîr-e mawlânâ jalâluddîn Muhammad mashhûr ba-mawlawî*, v. 582; Gölpinarli, *Dîvân-i Kebîr Mevlânâ Celâleddin*, 115, v. 410.

13. Can, *Hz. Mevlânâ'nin Rubâîleri*, v. 1732; Ergin, *Mevlânâ Celâleddin Rubâîler*, 364; Forûzânfar (ed.), *Kulliyât-é snams yâ dîwân-é kabîr-e mawlânâ jalâluddîn Muhammad mashhûr ba-mawlawî*, v. 1556; Gölpinarli, *Dîvân-i Kebîr Mevlânâ Celâleddin*, 193, v. 36.

14. Can, *Hz. Mevlânâ'nin Rubâîleri*, v. 1914; Ergin, *Mevlânâ Celâleddin Rubâîler*, 398; Forûzânfar (ed.), *Kulliyât-é snams yâ dîwân-é kabîr-e mawlânâ jalâluddîn Muhammad mashhûr ba-mawlawî*, 1918; Gölpinarli, *Dîvân-i Kebîr Mevlânâ Celâleddin*, 197, v. 3.

15. Can, *Hz. Mevlânâ'nin Rubâîleri*, v. 184; Ergin, *Mevlânâ Celâleddin Rubâîler*, 81; Forûzânfar (ed.), *Kulliyât-é snams yâ dîwân-é kabîr-e mawlânâ jalâluddîn Muhammad mashhûr ba-mawlawî*, v. 166; Gölpinarli, *Mevlânâ Celâleddin, Rubâîler*, T38, v. 91.

16. Can, *Hz. Mevlânâ'nin Rubâîleri*, v. 852; Ergin, *Mevlânâ Celâleddin Rubâîler*, 158; Forûzânfar (ed.), *Kulliyât-é snams yâ dîwân-é kabîr-e mawlânâ jalâluddîn Muhammad mashhûr ba-mawlawî*, v. 800; Gölpinarli, *Mevlânâ Celâleddin, Rubâîler*, D83, v. 138.

17. Can, *Hz. Mevlânâ'nin Rubâîleri*, v. 792; Ergin, *Mevlânâ Celâleddin*

Rubâîler, 159; Forûzânfar (ed.), *Kulliyât-é snams yâ dîwân-é kabîr-e mawlânâ jalâluddîn Muhammad mashhûr ba-mawlawî*, v. 739; Gölpinarli, *Mevlânâ Celâleddin, Rubâîler*, D71, v. 30.

18. Ergin, *Mevlânâ Celâleddin Rubâîler*, 178; Gölpinarli, *Mevlânâ Celâleddin, Rubâîler*, D109, v. 362.

19. Can, *Hz. Mevlânâ'nin Rubâîleri*, v. 799; Ergin, *Mevlânâ Celâleddin Rubâîler*, 200; Forûzânfar (ed.), *Kulliyât-é snams yâ dîwân-é kabîr-e mawlânâ jalâluddîn Muhammad mashhûr ba-mawlawî*, v. 746; Gölpinarli, *Mevlânâ Celâleddin, Rubâîler* D73, v. 49.

20. Can, *Hz. Mevlânâ'nin Rubâîleri*, v. 1537; Ergin, *Mevlânâ Celâleddin Rubâîler*, 332; Forûzânfar (ed.), *Kulliyât-é snams yâ dîwân-é kabîr-e mawlânâ jalâluddîn Muhammad mashhûr ba-mawlawî*, v. 1374; Gölpinarli, *Mevlânâ Celâleddin, Rubâîler*, N168, v. 12.

21. Can, *Hz. Mevlânâ'nin Rubâîleri*, v. 1936; Ergin, *Mevlânâ Celâleddin Rubâîler*, 397; Forûzânfar (ed.), *Kulliyât-é snams yâ dîwân-é kabîr-e mawlânâ jalâluddîn Muhammad mashhûr ba-mawlawî*, v. 1743; Gölpinarli, *Mevlânâ Celâleddin, Rubâîler*, Y199, v. 13.

PART 5. ON RELIGION

1. Yonsel, *Tasavvfundan Derinliklerinde Bir Gezinti*, 21.

2. Shushud, *Hâcegân Hânedâni*, 139; Shushud, *Masters of Wisdom of Central Asia*, 133.

3. Yonsel, *Tasavvfundan Derinliklerinde Bir Gezinti*, 26.

4. Ibid., 61.

5. Ibid., 43.

6. Ibid., 62.

7. Ibid., 58.

8. Ibid., 69.

9. Ibid., 58.

10. Ibid., 11.

11. Ibid., 58.

12. Can, *Hz. Mevlânâ'nin Rubâîleri*, v. 856; Ergin, *Mevlânâ Celâleddin Rubâîler*, 16; Forûzânfar (ed.), *Kulliyât-é snams yâ dîwân-é kabîr-e mawlânâ jalâluddîn Muhammad mashhûr ba-mawlawî*, v. 804; Gölpinarli, *Dîvân-i Kebîr Mevlânâ Celâleddin*, 83, v. 140.

13. Can, *Hz. Mevlânâ'nin Rubâîleri*, v. 821; Ergin, *Mevlânâ Celâleddin Rubâîler*, 197; Forûzânfar (ed.), *Kulliyât-é snams yâ dîwân-é kabîr-e mawlânâ jalâluddîn Muhammad mashhûr ba-mawlawî*, v. 768; Gölpinarli, *Mevlânâ Celâleddin, Rubâîler*, D91, v. 206.

14. Can, *Hz. Mevlânâ'nin Rubâîleri*, v. 1776; Ergin, *Mevlânâ Celâleddin Rubâîler*, 387; Forûzânfar (ed.), *Kulliyât-é snams yâ dîwân-é kabîr-e mawlânâ jalâluddîn Muhammad mashhûr ba-mawlawî*, v. 1591; Gölpinarli, *Mevlânâ Celâleddin, Rubâîler*, H183, v. 29.

PART 6. ON PERCEPTION

1. Shushud, *Hâcegân Hânedâni*, 136; Shushud, *Masters of Wisdom of Central Asia*, 131.

2. Yonsel, *Tasavvfundan Derinliklerinde Bir Gezinti*, 41.

3. Ibid., 66.

4. Shushud, *Hâcegân Hânedâni*, 30; Shushud, *Masters of Wisdom of Central Asia*, 128.

5. Shushud, *Hâcegân Hânedâni*, 157; Shushud, *Masters of Wisdom of Central Asia*, 151.

6. Can, *Hz. Mevlânâ'nin Rubâîleri*, v. 577; Ergin, *Mevlânâ Celâleddin Rubâîler*, 207; Forûzânfar (ed.), *Kulliyât-é snams yâ dîwân-é kabîr-e mawlânâ jalâluddîn Muhammad mashhûr ba-mawlawî*, v. 522; Gölpinarli, *Dîvân-i Kebîr Mevlânâ Celâleddin*, 114, v. 406.

7. Can, *Hz. Mevlânâ'nin Rubâîleri*, v. 969; Ergin, *Mevlânâ Celâleddin Rubâîler*, 208; Gölpinarli, *Dîvân-i Kebîr Mevlânâ Celâleddin*, 115, v. 409.

8. Can, *Hz. Mevlânâ'nin Rubâîleri*, v. 519; Ergin, *Mevlânâ Celâleddin Rubâîler*, 214; Forûzânfar (ed.), *Kulliyât-é snams yâ dîwân-é kabîr-e mawlânâ jalâluddîn Muhammad mashhûr ba-mawlawî*, v. 464; Gölpinarli, *Mevlânâ Celâleddin, Rubâîler*, D94, v. 235.

9. Ergin, *Dîvân-i Kebîr of Mevlânâ Celâleddin Rumi, Meter 4*, 181–82, v. 3483–84, 3487–88.

10. Ergin, *Dîvân-i Kebîr of Mevlânâ Celâleddin Rumi, Meter 22*, 149, v. 635.

11. Ibid., 46, v. 619.

12. Gölpinarli, *Dîvân-i Kebîr Mevlânâ Celâleddin*, 391.

13. Shushud, *Masters of Wisdom of Central Asia*, 138.

14. Gölpinarli, *Dîvân-i Kebîr Mevlânâ Celâleddin*.

15. Ergin, *Dîvân-i Kebîr of Mevlânâ Celâleddin Rumi*, Meter 10, 152, v. 737.

16. Ergin, *Dîvân-i Kebîr of Mevlânâ Celâleddin Rumi*, Meter 8b, 191, v. 1961.

17. Gölpinarli, *Dîvân-i Kebîr Mevlânâ Celâleddin*.

18. Ibid., 391.

19. Ibid., 617.

20. Ergin, *Dîvân-i Kebîr of Mevlânâ Celâleddin Rumi*, Meter 19, 72, v. 2473.

21. Gölpinarli, *Dîvân-i Kebîr Mevlânâ Celâleddin*.

22. Ibid., 162.

23. Ibid.

24. Ibid., 541.

PART 7. ON DEATH

1. Yonsel, *Tasavvfundan Derinliklerinde Bir Gezinti*, 47.

2. Shushud, *Hâcegân Hânedâni*, 156; Shushud, *Masters of Wisdom of Central Asia*, 149.

3. Shushud, *Fakir Sözleri (Itlâk Tasavvufundan Lâtifeler)*, 16.

4. Yonsel, *Tasavvfundan Derinliklerinde Bir Gezinti*, 19.

5. Ibid., 44.

6. Shushud, *Hâcegân Hânedâni*, 156; Shushud, *Masters of Wisdom of Central Asia*, 148.

7. Can, *Hz. Mevlânâ'nin Rubâîleri*, v. 1030; Forûzânfar (ed.), *Kulliyât-é snams yâ dîwân-é kabîr-e mawlânâ jalâluddîn Muhammad mashhûr ba-mawlawî*, v. 922; Gölpinarli, *Dîvân-i Kebîr Mevlânâ Celâleddin*, 119, v. 13.

8. Can, *Hz. Mevlânâ'nin Rubâîleri*, v. 1074; Forûzânfar (ed.), *Kulliyât-é snams yâ dîwân-é kabîr-e mawlânâ jalâluddîn Muhammad mashhûr ba-mawlawî*, v. 959; Gölpinarli, *Dîvân-i Kebîr Mevlânâ Celâleddin*, 123, v. 15.

9. Can, *Hz. Mevlânâ'nin Rubâîleri*, v. 423; Ergin, *Mevlânâ Celâleddin Rubâîler*, 59; Forûzânfar (ed.), *Kulliyât-é snams yâ dîwân-é kabîr-e mawlânâ jalâluddîn Muhammad mashhûr ba-mawlawî*, v. 405; Gölpinarli, *Dîvân-i Kebîr Mevlânâ Celâleddin*, 33, v. 50.

10. Can, *Hz. Mevlânâ'nin Rubâîleri*, v. 331; Ergin, *Mevlânâ Celâleddin Rubâîler*, 80; Forûzânfar (ed.), *Kulliyât-é snams yâ dîwân-é kabîr-e mawlânâ jalâluddîn Muhammad mashhûr ba-mawlawî*, v. 313; Gölpinarli, *Dîvân-i Kebîr Mevlânâ Celâleddin*, 38, v. 90.

11. Gölpinarli, *Dîvân-i Kebîr Mevlânâ Celâleddin.*

12. Can, *Hz. Mevlânâ'nin Rubâîleri,* v. 1594; Ergin, *Mevlânâ Celâleddin Rubâîler,* 358; Forûzânfar (ed.), *Kulliyât-é snams yâ dîwân-é kabîr-e mawlânâ jalâluddîn Muhammad mashhûr ba-mawlawî,* 1431; Gölpinarli, *Mevlânâ Celâleddin, Rubâîler,* N174, v. 59.

PART 8. ON LIFE

1. Shushud, *Hâcegân Hânedâni,* 126; Shushud, *Masters of Wisdom of Central Asia,* 124.

2. Yonsel, *Tasavvfundan Derinliklerinde Bir Gezinti,* 12.

3. Ibid., 44.

4. Ibid., 64.

5. Ibid., 56.

6. Ibid.

7. Ibid., 50.

8. Ibid., 55.

9. Ibid., 29.

10. Can, *Hz. Mevlânâ'nin Rubâileri,* v. 505; Forûzänfar (ed.), *Kulliyât-é snams yâ dîwân-é kabîr-e mawlânâ jalâluddîn Muhammad mashhûr ba-mawlawî,* v. 450; Gölpinarli, *Dîvân-i Kebîr Mevlânâ Celâleddin,* 102, v. 302.

11. Can, *Hz. Mevlânâ'nin Rubâileri,* v. 1721; Forûzänfar (ed.), *Kulliyât-é snams yâ dîwân-é kabîr-e mawlânâ jalâluddîn Muhammad mashhûr ba-mawlawî,* v. 1545; Gölpinarli, *Dîvân-i Kebîr Mevlânâ Celâleddin,* 193.

12. Ergin, *Dîvân-i Kebîr of Mevlânâ Celâleddin Rumi, Meter 19,* 72, v. 2473.

13. Can, *Hz. Mevlânâ'nin Rubâîleri,* v. 783; Ergin, *Mevlânâ Celâleddin Rubâîler,* 194; Forûzânfar (ed.), *Kulliyât-é snams yâ dîwân-é kabîr-e mawlânâ jalâluddîn Muhammad mashhûr ba-mawlawî,* v. 730; Gölpinarli, *Dîvân-i Kebîr Mevlânâ Celâleddin,* 72, v. 47.

PART 9. ON SUFFERING

1. Shushud, personal communication recorded in 1963.

2. Hasan Dede, www.hasandede.de, accessed November 5, 2013.

3. Shushud, *Masters of Wisdom of Central Asia,* 4.

4. Ibid., 145.

5. Ibid., 156.

6. Ibid.

7. Ibid.

8. Can, *Hz. Mevlânâ'nin Rubâîleri*, v. 1981; Forûzânfar (ed.), *Kulliyât-é snams yâ dîwân-é kabîr-e mawlânâ jalâluddîn Muhammad mashhûr ba-mawlawî*, v. 1788; Gölpinarli, *Dîvân-i Kebîr Mevlânâ Celâleddin*, 201, v. 36.

9. Ergin, *Dîvân-i Kebîr of Mevlânâ Celâleddin Rumi, Meter 2*, 150, v. 2842–53.

PART 10. ON BEING AND BECOMING

1. Shushud, *Hâcegân Hânedâni*, 142; Shushud, *Masters of Wisdom of Central Asia*, 138.

2. Yonsel, *Tasavvfundan Derinliklerinde Bir Gezinti*, 14.

3. Ibid., 58.

4. Ibid., 27.

5. Ibid., 35.

6. Ibid., 45.

7. Ibid., 36.

8. Ibid., 17.

9. Shushud, *Hâcegân Hânedâni*, 137; Shushud, *Masters of Wisdom of Central Asia*, 130.

10. Shushud, *Fakir Sözleri (Itlâk Tasavvufundan Lâtifeler)*, 16.

11. Shushud, *Masters of Wisdom of Central Asia*, 155.

12. Yonsel, *Tasavvfundan Derinliklerinde Bir Gezinti*, 34.

13. Shushud, *Hâcegân Hânedâni*, 140; Shushud, *Masters of Wisdom of Central Asia*, 134.

14. Shushud, *Hâcegân Hânedâni*, 141; Shushud, *Masters of Wisdom of Central Asia*, 134–35.

15. Shushud, *Hâcegân Hânedâni*, 143; Shushud, *Masters of Wisdom of Central Asia*, 138.

16. Can, *Hz. Mevlânâ'nin Rubâîleri*, v. 720; Ergin, *Mevlânâ Celâleddin Rubâîler*, 134; Forûzânfar (ed.), *Kulliyât-é snams yâ dîwân-é kabîr-e mawlânâ jalâluddîn Muhammad mashhûr ba-mawlawî*, v. 666; Gölpinarli, *Dîvân-i Kebîr Mevlânâ Celâleddin*, 67, v. 1.

17. Can, *Hz. Mevlânâ'nin Rubâîleri*, v. 788; Ergin, *Mevlânâ Celâleddin*

Rubâîler, 129; Forûzânfar (ed.), *Kulliyât-é snams yâ dîwân-é kabîr-e mawlânâ jalâluddîn Muhammad mashhûr ba-mawlawî,* v. 735; Gölpinarli, *Dîvân-i Kebîr Mevlânâ Celâleddin,* 68, v. 8.

18. Can, *Hz. Mevlânâ'nin Rubâîleri,* v. 1111; Ergin, *Mevlânâ Celâleddin Rubâîler,* 245; Forûzânfar (ed.), *Kulliyât-é snams yâ dîwân-é kabîr-e mawlânâ jalâluddîn Muhammad mashhûr ba-mawlawî,* v. 989; Gölpinarli, *Mevlânâ Celâleddin, Rubâîler,* 126, v. 10.

19. Can, *Hz. Mevlânâ'nin Rubâîleri,* v. 1432; Ergin, *Mevlânâ Celâleddin Rubâîler,* 301; Forûzânfar (ed.), *Kulliyât-é snams yâ dîwân-é kabîr-e mawlânâ jalâluddîn Muhammad mashhûr ba-mawlawî,* v. 1295; Gölpinarli, *Dîvân-i Kebîr Mevlânâ Celâleddin,* 162, v. 196.

20. Can, *Hz. Mevlânâ'nin Rubâîleri,* v. 244; Ergin, *Mevlânâ Celâleddin Rubâîler,* 80; Forûzânfar (ed.), *Kulliyât-é snams yâ dîwân-é kabîr-e mawlânâ jalâluddîn Muhammad mashhûr ba-mawlawî,* v. 226; Gölpinarli, *Dîvân-i Kebîr Mevlânâ Celâleddin,* 38, v. 89.

21. Can, *Hz. Mevlânâ'nin Rubâîleri,* v. 1752; Ergin, *Mevlânâ Celâleddin Rubâîler,* 372; Forûzânfar (ed.), *Kulliyât-é snams yâ dîwân-é kabîr-e mawlânâ jalâluddîn Muhammad mashhûr ba-mawlawî,* v. 1576; Gölpinarli, *Dîvân-i Kebîr Mevlânâ Celâleddin,* 191, v. 19.

22. Can, *Hz. Mevlânâ'nin Rubâîleri,* v. 505; Forûzânfar (ed.), *Kulliyât-é snams yâ dîwân-é kabîr-e mawlânâ jalâluddîn Muhammad mashhûr ba-mawlawî,* v. 450; Gölpinarli, *Dîvân-i Kebîr Mevlânâ Celâleddin,* 121, v. 102–302.

23. Can, *Hz. Mevlânâ'nin Rubâîleri,* v. 519; Forûzânfar (ed.), *Kulliyât-é snams yâ dîwân-é kabîr-e mawlânâ jalâluddîn Muhammad mashhûr ba-mawlawî,* v. 464; Gölpinarli, *Dîvân-i Kebîr Mevlânâ Celâleddin,* 214, v. 94–235.

24. Can, *Hz. Mevlânâ'nin Rubâîleri,* v. 372; Ergin, *Mevlânâ Celâleddin Rubâîler,* 85; Forûzânfar (ed.), *Kulliyât-é snams yâ dîwân-é kabîr-e mawlânâ jalâluddîn Muhammad mashhûr ba-mawlawî,* v. 354; Gölpinarli, *Mevlânâ Celâleddin, Rubâîler,* T39, v. 101.

25. Can, *Hz. Mevlânâ'nin Rubâîleri,* v. 515; Ergin, *Mevlânâ Celâleddin Rubâîler,* 148; Forûzânfar (ed.), *Kulliyât-é snams yâ dîwân-é kabîr-e mawlânâ jalâluddîn Muhammad mashhûr ba-mawlawî,* 460; Gölpinarli, *Mevlânâ Celâleddin, Rubâîler,* D105, v. 326.

26. Shushud, personal communication recorded in 1963.

27. Ibid.

28. Ibid.

29. Ibid.

30. Gölpinarli, *Mevlânâ Celâleddin, Rubâîler,* 193, v. 35.

31. Shushud, personal communication recorded in 1963.

PART 11. ON LOVE

1. Shushud, *Hâcegân Hânedâni,* 120; Shushud, *Masters of Wisdom of Central Asia,* 127.

2. Yonsel, *Tasavvfundan Derinliklerinde Bir Gezinti,* 57.

3. Ibid., 47.

4. Can, *Hz. Mevlânâ'nin Rubâîleri,* v. 343; Ergin, *Mevlânâ Celâleddin Rubâîler,* 92; Forûzânfar (ed.), *Kulliyât-é snams yâ dîwân-é kabîr-e mawlânâ jalâluddîn Muhammad mashhûr ba-mawlawî,* v. 325; Gölpinarli, *Dîvân-i Kebîr Mevlânâ Celâleddin,* 41, v. 114.

5. Can, *Hz. Mevlânâ'nin Rubâîleri,* v. 769; Ergin, *Mevlânâ Celâleddin Rubâîler,* 165; Forûzânfar (ed.), *Kulliyât-é snams yâ dîwân-é kabîr-e mawlânâ jalâluddîn Muhammad mashhûr ba-mawlawî,* v. 715; Gölpinarli, *Dîvân-i Kebîr Mevlânâ Celâleddin,* 84, v. 149.

6. Can, *Hz. Mevlânâ'nin Rubâîleri,* v. 225; Ergin, *Mevlânâ Celâleddin Rubâîler,* 103; Forûzânfar (ed.), *Kulliyât-é snams yâ dîwân-é kabîr-e mawlânâ jalâluddîn Muhammad mashhûr ba-mawlawî,* v. 225; Gölpinarli, *Dîvân-i Kebîr Mevlânâ Celâleddin,* 44, v. 139.

7. Can, *Hz. Mevlânâ'nin Rubâîleri,* v. 647; Ergin, *Mevlânâ Celâleddin Rubâîler,* 176; Forûzânfar (ed.), *Kulliyât-é snams yâ dîwân-é kabîr-e mawlânâ jalâluddîn Muhammad mashhûr ba-mawlawî,* v. 593; Gölpinarli, *Dîvân-i Kebîr Mevlânâ Celâleddin,* 86, v. 169.

8. Can, *Hz. Mevlânâ'nin Rubâîleri,* v. 1148; Ergin, *Mevlânâ Celâleddin Rubâîler,* 251; Forûzânfar (ed.), *Kulliyât-é snams yâ dîwân-é kabîr-e mawlânâ jalâluddîn Muhammad mashhûr ba-mawlawî,* v. 1024; Gölpinarli, *Dîvân-i Kebîr Mevlânâ Celâleddin,* 128, v. 21.

9. Can, *Hz. Mevlânâ'nin Rubâîleri,* v. 1306; Ergin, *Mevlânâ Celâleddin Rubâîler,* 307; Forûzânfar (ed.), *Kulliyât-é snams yâ dîwân-é kabîr-e mawlânâ jalâluddîn Muhammad mashhûr ba-mawlawî,* v. 1168; Gölpinarli, *Dîvân-i Kebîr Mevlânâ Celâleddin,* 162, v. 201.

10. Ergin, *Dîvân-i Kebîr of Mevlânâ Celâleddin Rumi, Meter 5, 6, 7a,* 94, v. 32.

11. Ergin, *Dîvân-i Kebîr of Mevlânâ Celâleddin Rumi, Meter 11,* 154, v. 968.

12. Ergin, *Dîvân-i Kebîr of Mevlânâ Celâleddin Rumi, Meter 14,* 76, v. 1774.

13. Ergin, *Dîvân-i Kebîr of Mevlânâ Celâleddin Rumi*, Meter 5, 6, 7a, 3, v. 10.

14. Ergin, *Dîvân-i Kebîr of Mevlânâ Celâleddin Rumi*, Meter 7, 190, v. 2868.

15. Ergin, *Dîvân-i Kebîr of Mevlânâ Celâleddin Rumi*, Meter 11, 72, v. 424.

16. Can, *Hz. Mevlânâ'nin Rubâîleri*, v. 344; Ergin, *Mevlânâ Celâleddin Rubâîler*, 62; Forûzânfar (ed.), *Kulliyât-é snams yâ dîwân-é kabîr-e mawlânâ jalâluddîn Muhammad mashhûr ba-mawlawî*, v. 326; Gölpinarli, *Mevlânâ Celâleddin, Rubâîler*, T55, v. 229.

17. Can, *Hz. Mevlânâ'nin Rubâîleri*, v. 281; Ergin, *Mevlânâ Celâleddin Rubâîler*, 79; Forûzânfar (ed.), *Kulliyât-é snams yâ dîwân-é kabîr-e mawlânâ jalâluddîn Muhammad mashhûr ba-mawlawî*, v. 263; Gölpinarli, *Mevlânâ Celâleddin, Rubâîler*, T38, v. 85.

18. Can, *Hz. Mevlânâ'nin Rubâîleri*, v. 504; Ergin, *Mevlânâ Celâleddin Rubâîler*, 197; Forûzânfar (ed.), *Kulliyât-é snams yâ dîwân-é kabîr-e mawlânâ jalâluddîn Muhammad mashhûr ba-mawlawî*, v. 449; Gölpinarli, *Mevlânâ Celâleddin, Rubâîler*, D113, v. 391.

19. Can, *Hz. Mevlânâ'nin Rubâîleri*, v. 611; Ergin, *Mevlânâ Celâleddin Rubâîler*, 198; Forûzânfar (ed.), *Kulliyât-é snams yâ dîwân-é kabîr-e mawlânâ jalâluddîn Muhammad mashhûr ba-mawlawî*, v. 556; Gölpinarli, *Mevlânâ Celâleddin, Rubâîler*, D91, v. 211.

20. Can, *Hz. Mevlânâ'nin Rubâîleri*, v. 807; Ergin, *Mevlânâ Celâleddin Rubâîler*, 198; Forûzânfar (ed.), *Kulliyât-é snams yâ dîwân-é kabîr-e mawlânâ jalâluddîn Muhammad mashhûr ba-mawlawî*, v. 754; Gölpinarli, *Mevlânâ Celâleddin, Rubâîler*, D91, v. 210.

21. Can, *Hz. Mevlânâ'nin Rubâîleri*, v. 555; Ergin, *Mevlânâ Celâleddin Rubâîler*, 199; Forûzânfar (ed.), *Kulliyât-é snams yâ dîwân-é kabîr-e mawlânâ jalâluddîn Muhammad mashhûr ba-mawlawî*, v. 500; Gölpinarli, *Mevlânâ Celâleddin, Rubâîler*, D73, v. 51.

22. Can, *Hz. Mevlânâ'nin Rubâîleri*, v. 753; Ergin, *Mevlânâ Celâleddin Rubâîler*, 199; Forûzânfar (ed.), *Kulliyât-é snams yâ dîwân-é kabîr-e mawlânâ jalâluddîn Muhammad mashhûr ba-mawlawî*, v. 699; Gölpinarli, *Mevlânâ Celâleddin, Rubâîler*, D91, v. 208.

23. Can, *Hz. Mevlânâ'nin Rubâîleri*, v. 836; Ergin, *Mevlânâ Celâleddin Rubâîler*, 214; Forûzânfar (ed.), *Kulliyât-é snams yâ dîwân-é kabîr-e mawlânâ jalâluddîn Muhammad mashhûr ba-mawlawî*, v. 784; Gölpinarli, *Mevlânâ Celâleddin, Rubâîler*, D116, v. 415.

24. Can, *Hz. Mevlânâ'nin Rubâîleri*, v. 1110; Ergin, *Mevlânâ Celâleddin Rubâîler*, 244; Forûzânfar (ed.), *Kulliyât-é snams yâ dîwân-é kabîr-e*

mawlânâ jalâluddîn Muhammad mashhûr ba-mawlawî, v. 988; Gölpinarli, *Mevlânâ Celâleddin, Rubâîler,* S125, v. 7.

25. Can, *Hz. Mevlânâ'nin Rubâîleri,* v. 1111; Ergin, *Mevlânâ Celâleddin Rubâîler,* 245; Forûzânfar (ed.), *Kulliyât-é snams yâ dîwân-é kabîr-e mawlânâ jalâluddîn Muhammad mashhûr ba-mawlawî,* v. 989; Gölpinarli, *Mevlânâ Celâleddin, Rubâîler,* S126, v. 10.

26. Can, *Hz. Mevlânâ'nin Rubâîleri,* v. 1179; Ergin, *Mevlânâ Celâleddin Rubâîler,* 257; Forûzânfar (ed.), *Kulliyât-é snams yâ dîwân-é kabîr-e mawlânâ jalâluddîn Muhammad mashhûr ba-mawlawî,* v. 1048; Gölpinarli, *Mevlânâ Celâleddin, Rubâîler,* A2–131, v. 3.

27. Ergin, *Mevlânâ Celâleddin Rubâîler,* 262; Gölpinarli, *Mevlânâ Celâleddin, Rubâîler,* K339–134, v. 6.

28. Can, *Hz. Mevlânâ'nin Rubâîleri,* v. 1232; Ergin, *Mevlânâ Celâleddin Rubâîler,* 266; Forûzânfar (ed.), *Kulliyât-é snams yâ dîwân-é kabîr-e mawlânâ jalâluddîn Muhammad mashhûr ba-mawlawî,* v. 1098; Gölpinarli, *Mevlânâ Celâleddin, Rubâîler,* L329–137, v. 17.

29. Can, *Hz. Mevlânâ'nin Rubâîleri,* v. 1614; Ergin, *Mevlânâ Celâleddin Rubâîler,* 338; Forûzânfar (ed.), *Kulliyât-é snams yâ dîwân-é kabîr-e mawlânâ jalâluddîn Muhammad mashhûr ba-mawlawî,* v. 1451; Gölpinarli, *Mevlânâ Celâleddin, Rubâîler,* N176, v. 26.

30. Can, *Hz. Mevlânâ'nin Rubâîleri,* v. 1678; Ergin, *Mevlânâ Celâleddin Rubâîler,* 346; Forûzânfar (ed.), *Kulliyât-é snams yâ dîwân-é kabîr-e mawlânâ jalâluddîn Muhammad mashhûr ba-mawlawî,* v. 1515; Gölpinarli, *Mevlânâ Celâleddin, Rubâîler,* N172, v. 49.

31. Can, *Hz. Mevlânâ'nin Rubâîleri,* v. 1539; Ergin, *Mevlânâ Celâleddin Rubâîler,* 348; Forûzânfar (ed.), *Kulliyât-é snams yâ dîwân-é kabîr-e mawlânâ jalâluddîn Muhammad mashhûr ba-mawlawî,* v. 1376; Gölpinarli, *Mevlânâ Celâleddin, Rubâîler,* N177, v. 90.

32. Can, *Hz. Mevlânâ'nin Rubâîleri,* v. 1648; Ergin, *Mevlânâ Celâleddin Rubâîler,* 355; Forûzânfar (ed.), *Kulliyât-é snams yâ dîwân-é kabîr-e mawlânâ jalâluddîn Muhammad mashhûr ba-mawlawî,* v. 1485; Gölpinarli, *Mevlânâ Celâleddin, Rubâîler,* N175, v. 68.

33. Can, *Hz. Mevlânâ'nin Rubâîleri,* v. 1793; Ergin, *Mevlânâ Celâleddin Rubâîler,* 377; Forûzânfar (ed.), *Kulliyât-é snams yâ dîwân-é kabîr-e mawlânâ jalâluddîn Muhammad mashhûr ba-mawlawî,* v. 1608; Gölpinarli, *Mevlânâ Celâleddin, Rubâîler,* H181, v. 9.

34. Ergin, *Dîvân-i Kebîr of Mevlânâ Celâleddin Rumi, Meter 9,* 43, v. 257.

35. Gölpinarli, *Dîvân-i Kebîr Mevlânâ Celâleddin,* 594.

36. Ibid.

37. Ergin, *Dîvân-i Kebîr of Mevlânâ Celâleddin Rumi, Meter 11,* 154, v. 968.

38. Ergin, *Dîvân-i Kebîr of Mevlânâ Celâleddin Rumi, Meter 5, 6, 7a,* 94, v. 32.

39. Ergin, *Dîvân-i Kebîr of Mevlânâ Celâleddin Rumi, Meter 10.*

40. Gölpinarli, *Dîvân-i Kebîr Mevlânâ Celâleddin.*

41. Shushud, *Masters of Wisdom of Central Asia,* 155.

A STORY: TWO PLACES AT ONCE

1. Yonsel, *Tasavvfundan Derinliklerinde Bir Gezinti,* 58.

ABOUT THE AUTHORS

1. Ergin, *Dîvân-i Kebîr of Mevlânâ Celâleddin Rumi, Meter 5, 6, 7a,* 65, v. 134–144.

2. Gölpinarli, *Dîvân-i Kebîr Mevlânâ Celâleddin.*

3. Ibid.

4. Ibid.

5. Ibid.

6. Ibid.

7. Ibid.

8. Ibid.

9. Ibid.

10. Ibid., 600.

Bibliography

Can, Şefik. *Hz. Mevlânâ'nin Rubâîleri*. Ankara, Turkey: T. C. Kûltûr Bakanliği Yayinlari/2752 Yayimlar Dairesi Başkanliği Sanat-Ebediyat Eserleri Dizise/3655–120, 2001.

Ergin, Nevit. *Dîvân-i Kebîr of Mevlânâ Celâleddin Rumi, Meter 1*. Los Angeles: Echo Publications, 1995.

———. *Dîvân-i Kebîr of Mevlânâ Celâleddin Rumi, Meter 2*. Los Angeles: Echo Publications, 1995.

———. *Dîvân-i Kebîr of Mevlânâ Celâleddin Rumi, Meter 4*. Los Angeles: Echo Publications, 1996.

———. *Dîvân-i Kebîr of Mevlânâ Celâleddin Rumi, Meter 5, 6, 7a*. Los Angeles: Echo Publications, 1997.

———. *Dîvân-i Kebîr of Mevlânâ Celâleddin Rumi, Meter 7*. Los Angeles: Echo Publications, 1997.

———. *Dîvân-i Kebîr of Mevlânâ Celâleddin Rumi, Meter 8a*. Los Angeles: Echo Publications, 1998.

———. *Dîvân-i Kebîr of Mevlânâ Celâleddin Rumi, Meter 8b*. Los Angeles: Echo Publications, 1998.

———. *Dîvân-i Kebîr of Mevlânâ Celâleddin Rumi, Meter 9*. Los Angeles: Echo Publications, 1999.

———. *Dîvân-i Kebîr of Mevlânâ Celâleddin Rumi, Meter 10*. Los Angeles: Echo Publications, 2000.

———. *Dîvân-i Kebîr of Mevlânâ Celâleddin Rumi, Meter 11*. Los Angeles: Echo Publications, 2000.

———. *Dîvân-i Kebîr of Mevlânâ Celâleddin Rumi, Meter 12*. Los Angeles: Echo Publications, 2000.

———. *Dîvân-i Kebîr of Mevlânâ Celâleddin Rumi, Meter 14.* Los Angeles: Echo Publications, 2001.

———. *Dîvân-i Kebîr of Mevlânâ Celâleddin Rumi, Meter 18.* Los Angeles: Echo Publications, 2002.

———. *Dîvân-i Kebîr of Mevlânâ Celâleddin Rumi, Meter 19.* Los Angeles: Echo Publications, 2002.

———. *Dîvân-i Kebîr of Mevlânâ Celâleddin Rumi, Meter 22.* Los Angeles: Echo Publications, 2003.

———. *Mevlânâ Celâleddin Rubâîler.* Los Angeles: Echo Publications, 2013.

Forûzânfar, Badî'uzzamân, ed. *Kulliyât-é snams yâ dîwân-é kabîr-e mawlânâ jalâluddîn Muhammad mashhûr ba-mawlawî.* Tehrân, Iran: University of Tehrân, 1957–1967.

Gölpinarli, Abdülbâki. *Dîvân-i Kebîr Mevlânâ Celâleddin.* I–VII. Ankara: Turkey: Kültür Bakanliği, 1992.

———. *Mevlânâ Celâleddin, Rubâîler.* Ankara: Turkey: Ajans-Türk Matbaacilik Sanayî, 1982.

Shushud, Hasan Lutfi. *Fakir Sözleri (Itlâk Tasavvufundan Lâtifeler).* Istanbul, Turkey: Doğan Kardeş Yayinlri A. Ş. Basimevi, 1958.

———. *Hâcegân Hânedâni.* Istanbul, Turkey: Doğan Kardeş Yayinlri A. Ş. Basimevi, 1958b.

———. *Masters of Wisdom of Central Asia.* Translated by Muhtar Holland. Moorcote, England: Combe Springs Press, 1983.

Yonsel, Melih. *Tasavvufundan Derinliklerinde Bir Gezinti.* Istanbul, Turkey: Baski: Yaşar Matbassi, 1996.

BOOKS OF RELATED INTEREST

Tales of a Modern Sufi
The Invisible Fence of Reality and Other Stories
by Nevit O. Ergin

The Forbidden Rumi
The Suppressed Poems of Rumi on Love, Heresy, and Intoxication
Translations and Commentary by Nevit O. Ergin and Will Johnson

The Rubais of Rumi
Insane with Love
Translations and Commentary by Nevit O. Ergin and Will Johnson

The Spiritual Practices of Rumi
Radical Techniques for Beholding the Divine
by Will Johnson

Rumi's Four Essential Practices
Ecstatic Body, Awakened Soul
by Will Johnson

Muhammad
His Life Based on the Earliest Sources
by Martin Lings

Sufi Rapper
The Spiritual Journey of Abd al Malik
by Abd al Malik

The Cosmic Script
Sacred Geometry and the Science of Arabic Penmanship
by Ahmed Moustafa and Stefan Sperl

INNER TRADITIONS • BEAR & COMPANY
P.O. Box 388
Rochester, VT 05767
1-800-246-8648
www.InnerTraditions.com

Or contact your local bookseller